Christianity Terminated

T. G. WILLIS

Ordering Information:

Prime Seven Media
518 Landmann St.
Tomah City, WI 54660

Printed in the United States of America

Preface

"A wealth of information creates a poverty of attention" said American political scientist Herbert Simon.[i] Western civilisation's attention has shallowed from more-focused Christian values to embrace minority opinions and traditions, technical possibilities, as well as reconfiguring masculine and feminine definitions. All this since reaching its moral peak arguably around 1950 CE. The subtle seduction of established values and morals is somewhat reminiscent of a cracked egg slowly oozing out of its shell into oblivion.

However, this is not unexpected and is contributing to the anticipated end of true Christianity. Albeit global religions will continue in their appeasing lie to dull the conscience.

It is from this premise I have written this book.

On a more personal note, born in Zimbabwe, I grew up in a church environment, and at the age of six, asked Jesus into my life, but it wasn't until I was twenty-six that I became aware of the reality of God's presence.

After a motor accident which threw me out of the car, landing headfirst onto rocks in the roadside ditch, and presumed dead, I spent three days unconscious in hospital, where soon after awakening, and finding there were no apparent broken bones, was subsequently discharged. Informed I would probably never walk again, resulting from brain, eyesight, and balance damage, was carried to my bed at home. I fasted and prayed, hoping and expecting that God would either heal me or I would die of starvation. With the prospect of being bedridden for the rest of my life, this seemed my only alternative, as I was only twenty-six.

On the third day of my fast I was given a book called 'Christ the Healer'[ii] and after reading it, had an inward, insistent urge to 'get up and walk'. I had no balance, but my legs were still strong, so I pushed myself up against the wall and began 'palming' myself along the wall until I could navigate around the house. Although unsteady on my feet, I finally walked unaided, but it took months. All the while I was learning to recognise God's voice personally speaking to me from the Bible and through my own conscience - always encouraging, always comforting.

Subsequently, I studied and dissected the Scripture's contents, paying attention to congruent topics and instructions, as well as expected eschatological matters, outlined in God's plan for humanity.

This recount is not designed to inspire response, but merely to demonstrate how God often uses misfortune and suffering to direct our lives, as we look forward to the termination of Christianity.

Introduction

After observing the sweeping changes of life's journey in one's own lifetime, it's a fascinating exercise to trace the progress of human civilization over the last century or so – even though the specific accuracy of much of it is limited to personal and relative experience of others. Subjective agendas, programs, and opinions are influencing news outlets more and more of late. In the aftermath of two world wars that engulfed most of the world's populations, monumental effects in the balance of family structure have occurred.

> **"World War I's impact on women's roles in society was immense. Women were conscripted to fill empty jobs left behind by the male servicemen, and as such, they were both idealized as symbols of the home front under attack and viewed with suspicion as their temporary freedom made them 'open to moral decay'."**[iii]

Women filled the vacated jobs of absent soldiers, which resulted in feminine values and foci altering, giving rise to feminist movements (such as the 'suffragettes') which began to demand higher respect in society. Then, UNICEF (United Nations Children's Fund) was formed in 1946 CE following the conclusion of the second world war. The focus of this organisation was on children's welfare, and, generally speaking, thereafter children were pampered and coddled to a greater degree, gradually promoting a less mature lifestyle, and an air of entitlement. Inadvertently, this also reduced restraint regarding self-discipline and moral values in spite of society encouraging individual performance and thought processes.

Films and television began to present a greater visual emphasis on younger and better-looking youth with a more casual point of view. Pop music groups flourished as musical preferences changed to a growing popular style. Gentle, soft 'elevator music' in telephones and shops has more recently been exchanged, largely for repetitive base percussion sounds with volume and 'beat', overcoming almost all other sonic styles relatively quickly.

Schools and universities gradually began to veer to the left in attitudes, evaluations, and demeanour. Education itself has become highly focused and complex in its desire for greater knowledge and know-how, although basic reading and writing skills have languished in many areas of the world. Traditionally, the task of a teacher has been to nourish the mind and help mould the character. Today we nourish the mind and encourage enlightened expediency to mould the character of our youth. The result, regarding law and order, is that the western nations have been forced to take relaxed attitudes – and this is not helpful to the security and stability of our societies.

The commercial release of the birth control pill, from 1960 CE, promoted choice for non-consequential sexual freedom, and proffered opportunities to effect stronger feminine influence in natural relationships. Apart from relaxing moral attitudes, this also promoted females into previously male-dominated areas of choice. Feminist movements began to thrive. The crippling effects of various drugs swept through the youth – especially in the Western world; production of drugs became more prolific in many nations as they grew economically. The previously established balance of life's flow began to destabilise and, like a rising river, feeling and prodding its banks, sought a new course to follow.

But an easy-going lifestyle has downfalls. For example, at this present time of writing, in America over 100,000 deaths have been attributed to the drug Tranq (the sedative Xylazine). 'Tranq' reduces a precious human being to a 'blob' with no control over either physical or mental faculties – and those are the fortunate ones! Additionally, attributed to Tranq, there have been many amputations of limbs which have become diseased and rotten.

Having given ourselves the right to decide on our own existence, the abortion of millions of human babies continues unabated. 'Right to life' issues are incessantly argued back and forth. It's strange how the more we focus on our own life and demand 'rights', the more unhappy we become. Actually, happiness is found in self-sacrifice and helping others![iv]

Similarly, our history, which has highlighted the godly importance of life by referring to chronological time as being BC (before Christ) and AD (after Christ), has more recently been overturned and is now cited as BCE (before Common Era) and CE (Common Era). The Christian influence on Western societies, in general, is declining.

This 'swing' in Western mindset was exacerbated with the advent of the personal computer. Around 1984 CE personal education and opinion on almost any subject inundated society via computer browsers, such as Google, Firefox, and Safari. In many ways this has diluted parental guidance and advice. Information became instant and apparently authoritative, often subjective, sometimes out-ranking hesitant, considered, parental remedies. This gave birth to what has been termed as 'the Millennial Generation' and was energised and supported by the growth of social platforms, such as Facebook and Twitter (or X as it now is).[v]

Politically, ancient, proven methods of leadership and government are slowly being jettisoned by youthful, relatively inexperienced representatives with bright new ideas that threaten established norms. They are endorsed by a growing majority of like-minded millennials! Throughout the world many governments are beginning to lean towards the left, endorsing and embracing hitherto-avoided policies, such as socialism and communism. Happiness seems more and more in demand, yet simultaneously is more and more elusive as we search for it in 'fun' activities.

Established moral values, that have been moulded and proven over many centuries, are currently morphing into strange and corrupt practises of selfishness and personal greed. These are comfortably accepted as normal business ethics in many circles. Being a 'man of your word' now seems quaint; a decisive handshake is no longer seen as 'sealing the deal'. More and more, when offered a handshake, an increasing number of young men respond with a limp, damp handshake akin to a wet fish, and do not deliver a 'grip' of re-assuring integrity and assurance. Even as feminism grows more robust in displaying masculine attributes, masculinity is being 'dumbed down' and being a strong male role-model has given way to a more effeminate demeanour.

Of course, none of the above is entirely new. The Bible records that, almost 3000 years ago, one of Israel's co-rulers, Queen Jezebel, for example, seized dominance over King Ahab, acted fraudulently and murderously towards all opposition, and when threatened, portrayed herself seductively attractive and surrounded herself with emasculated men – perhaps hoping to seduce or defeat her potential masculine competition? Aggressive women, effeminate men – same spirit, different times. But we are witnessing a marked increase in such practices. Yes, the above-mentioned behavioural aspects have always been part of humanity, but these characteristics are more recently exploding like a pot of expanding, boiling milk.

End of an Era

Various kingdoms and ideologies, throughout history, have subjugated certain populations and countries, forcing them to accept their own views. In modern history, a vile ideology in the form of Nazism assaulted the world and threatened to ultimately control most of the planet. Collective armies of countries that were opposed to Nazi conquest eventually overcame its murderous intent. A variety of oppressive regimes have, from time-to-time, temporarily controlled and decimated populations while pursuing their ideologies: such as North/South Korea, North/South Vietnam, the Soviet Union etc. Thankfully, more benign forces and countries have arisen to defend and defeat or, over time, at least counterbalance the evil galvanizing these oppressive actions.

However, in our current political circumstance there seems none to deliver the world order from the ridiculous extremist ideologies that are steadily eroding historically accepted lifestyles. Virtually the whole world is now being increasingly overtaken by the growing concepts of dreamers whose feet barely touch the ground! I believe that world opinion is currently gripped by strange new theories such as the deadly occurrence of methane flatulence and murderous climate change. A young Social Justice Warrior predicted the end of the world, as we know it, withing a handful of years. The Netherlands is in the process of removing 3000 farms to help manage the methane explosion affecting the health of the world.[vi] (I somehow doubt they asked God what He thinks! – or even China and India with populations of billions that rely on fossil fuels to exist.)

Coupled with that, the crypto-currency phenomenon remains open to manipulation, leaving many speculative investors vulnerable to devastating financial loss. Today financial security totters on the edge of an abyss, and even our own federal controls could be complicit in its downfall. The threatening possibilities are outlined by Geoff Remsburg:

"From this, the Fed (US Reserve Bank) **would have the ability to deposit funds directly into your account ... remove them ... apply new interest rates (possibly negative rates) ... deduct taxes and add refunds ... and whatever else it wanted, all in the blink of an eye."**[vii]

The growing reality of Artificial Intelligence appears destined to irreversibly change our lives. While we readily accept the benefits of GPS maps, computers and tracking, facial recognition, and others, it is alarming to hear contemplative ideas of manufacturing people and replacing human functions and interactions as announced by the Israeli historian, philosopher, and author Yuval Noah Harari[viii].

Having said all that, there is a faint chance that conservative thinkers, such as the American President Trump, the Canadian professor Jordan Peterson, the Israeli Prime Minister Benjamin Netanyahu, and many other influential people who attended the Alliance for Responsible Citizenship (ARC) conference in London, may briefly stave off the inevitability of questionable control of political policy for a while. But this possibility will not be permanent. The questions arise: did this general change in life's focus take God by surprise? How will he cope with this noticeable change of lifestyle direction?

Second Timothy states, **"For God saved us and called us to live a holy life. He did this, not because we deserved it, but because that was his plan from before the beginning of time-to show us his grace through Christ Jesus."**[ix]

Note! God had all history planned out! There is nothing happening today which God did not foresee before time began. Written nearly two thousand years ago, second Timothy chapter four 1-6 informs us of much of the attitudes and actions we see today. Malachi 3:6 records God emphasizing that he never changes his plan. Remarkably, the book of Revelation describes The Lamb (Jesus Christ) as being slain from the foundation of the world. We can therefore recognise that before life began, God anticipated every event and all things remain on expected track, due to terminate at God's chosen moment. Jesus said he would return to complete God's plan, and then time as we know it will end. Otherwise, no human would survive.[x] It's all in God's plan!

In other words, we are currently living in God's pre-conceived plan and expectations. For clearer understanding let the reader picture a tape measure that starts in your hand and stretches out of sight over the horizon. Imagine this extended tape represents eternity. Now, look at the first centimetre of the tape measure. The whole of history from the creation of the Earth until Christ's return is represented in this small section of the tape measure. Christianity's inception and finality were planned and measured before the earth's foundations were laid. The second centimetre will be a different story.

Examining current events, it would appear apparent that the whole world is in the grip of final destruction with no-one to come to the rescue. Only the promised return of Jesus Christ,[xi] will begin a new world order and way of life.

The obvious question springs to mind: Why would Christianity, a force that has immensely galvanised the global direction of humanity, suddenly terminate? When it does, what will become of humanity? Will it affect the physical earth? Simply answered, Christianity will have served its planned purpose, and the world will move into stage two of God's plan.

Included in Part 1
The Rise of Christianity

This first part of the book will outline how God selected a people to represent his intentions for mankind; how God introduced himself, with awesome display of might and power, to Moses highlighting moral principle and God's proposed, favoured intention. It also shows how, in response to Jewish recalcitrance, God amended his agreement with them when they spurned the integrity of the covenant; the debut of Christianity and how Christianity pared away from Judaism to Europe and the world; how God foretold the removal of the Church; how the Jews will come into prominence, and how the current purpose for the earth will finalise.

The layout of Part One:

1. **Jewish Beginnings**
    The Commencement of God's Plan
    Morality
    A separated group
    The Issues of God on Earth
    The Consequences of Choice
    End of the Line
    The New Direction
    Christianity Begins
2. **A Change of Track**
3. **Growth of Christianity in Europe and the Middle Ages**
4. **Christianity after the Middle Ages**
    History of Protestantism
    Christianity Expands
5. **Christianity in America**
6. **Grand Finale**
7. **In Closing**

The layout of

Part 2

God Loves you but...

This part dissects the gospel in detail and is dedicated to living life successfully; to line up with God's plan for a life of inexplicable peace and joy. It explains the reason for hardship (to the best of my understanding) and offers a vision for progressive life. It discusses the reason for the conscience and the perils of ignoring it. **When people do not accept divine guidance, they run wild.**[xii]

This life is the training ground for eternity beyond the first centimetre.

Part 1

Jewish Beginnings

The foundation of Christianity was laid with the revelation of God's personally delivered morals, originally revealed to Moses for God's specially chosen people, the Jews. This section of this book is a necessary part of the narrative because it highlights the development of moral principal, and God's reluctant distancing himself from his chosen people. This distancing resulted from the recalcitrance of the Jewish nation to comply in simple obedience, resulting finally in the advent of a new Covenant, the precursor to Christianity. Furthermore, this section reveals the influence and implementation of prescribed Godly morals that form the foundation of the Western Civilization.

Firstly, to establish a chronology of historic, biblical events: Nimrod, who was reputedly the most progressive man of his time, built the ancient city of Babylon. His recorded attributes were controlling people and hunting animals, perhaps to protect people. Now, as he also built several cities, principally Babylon, it seems quite reasonable that he may have been the designer and progenitor of the famed Tower of Babel, built around 2300 BCE which is apparently fairly close to the city of Babylon. Presumed archaeological ruins of the Tower of Babel indicate that the completed tower (estimated height 2485 m[xiii]) might have been nearly half the height of Mount Kilimanjaro, rendering breathing fairly challenging for the labourers. The Bible gives as a reason for building the tower to 'reach up into heaven and make a name [reputation] for ourselves'. Probably to be the 'leader group' amongst the people and to replace the invisible God with an alternative focal point. Whatever the reason, their pride and desire to reach or replace heaven's intention greatly angered God. He wiped it out supernaturally and confused the existing common language to end this humanly determined 'progressiveness' which lay outside God's own plan for humankind. God had powerfully intervened to issue a warning to future insurrectionists.

Now, the Tower of Babel is commonly regarded as a myth created to explain the multiplicity of today's human languages. However, it's uncanny how floods, towers, and a single universal language are found in the folk law, or creation stories of so many primitive populations around the world: Sumerian and Assyrian, Mexican, the original inhabitants of Arizona, Cherokee Indians, Nepalese, Batswana people, and so on. The presumed tower base is visible in southern Iraq. It might also be argued that this was the first recorded hierarchical structure. Over time, many towers and ziggurats were constructed for the sole purpose of becoming a religious or social focal point or structure to tower above its surroundings. e.g. the Eiffel Tower in Paris, France.

Contemporarily, the book of Genesis mentions the birth of the man, Peleg, in whose time the earth was geographically divided. While the Bible remains opaque regarding historical, physical, or geographical facts, to the Western mind, it might be presumed that this means God caused the tectonic plates of the earth to shift, thereby creating different continents and isolating like-identifying groups of people. With no specific details given, it is difficult to estimate time or circumstance achieving this. There is recorded in the Bible, how an earthquake occurred instantly, to remove an offending family, and other situations that boggle the natural mind.

The Commencement of God's plan for Christianity

Around 2000 BCE, and possibly overlapping Nimrod's lifespan, a man named Abram was born in the city of Ur (southern Iraq), some distance south of Babylon. At this time the Bible records that human longevity approximated two hundred years. Abram, later renamed Abraham, is considered the 'Father of Faith' to both Jewish and Christian religions, because of his unwavering faith in God and his actions. Although not specifically mentioned in the Bible, his father, Terah, is traditionally regarded as being an idol maker. Much greater attention was given to recognition of deity, in early history, than current understanding where experiential know-how has increased, and humanity is now persuaded to believe in its own destiny.

For some undisclosed reason, Terah decided to move from Ur, near the modern-day Persian Gulf, north to the city of Haran in Canaan, roughly on what is now the Syrian/Turkey border. He took his son Abram and grandson Lot with him. It was here that God chose Abram as his special focus for his plan for the earth. The Bible provides no special reason for God's choice. God delights in taking nobodies and making them into mighty people. God told Abram to cast loose his moorings from his father and begin following God's direction for his life. Therefore, at about the age of seventy-five, which was sixty years before his father's death, Abram departed with his wife Sarai and nephew Lot, plus livestock, to follow God's leading. God told Abram:

> "I will make you into a great nation, I will bless you and make you famous, and you will be a blessing to others. I will bless those who bless you and curse those who treat you with contempt. All families on earth will be blessed through you."[xiv]

Abram traversed the land of what is today Israel, from the very north down to Egypt. The two family members decided to go their separate ways at a certain point when, with their livestock growth, the herdsmen of Abram and Lot clashed over watering rights. Lot chose the fertile east and moved. God then spoke to Abram vowing that whatever Abram could see and wherever he had been would belong to him and his descendants, forever.

Around this time God began to reveal his attitude towards immoral and alternative practices.

By means of sulphur bombardment/meteor (often called brimstone), he destroyed the homosexual cities of Sodom and Gomorrah! Today, the barren, salt-stricken ruins of these cities is undergoing archaeologic investigation revealing sulphur fragments embedded in the surroundings which are being analysed. (There currently exist the remains of five cities that came under sulphuric destruction for immoral practices. The other three were named Admah, Zeboiim and Zoar (Bela)!)[xv]

Moses, who delivered Israel from slavery in Egypt, four generations later, referred to this debacle of the destroyed cities resulting in sulphur and salt remains, around 1400 BCE. In describing the remains of the cities, Moses brought Israel's attention to the folly of veering from God's personal care into ill-conceived ambition apart from God's prescription for life. This scenario contrasts God's transcendent plan of personal value against the socialistic plan of mass totalitarianism, which desires to erect its own parameters of living standards and values, and needs to know where you are, what you are planning, what you are thinking, and to govern your behaviour—for the assumed good of the people, of course! All other political 'isms' are likewise ridiculed by God. God will not share his glory with anyone.[xvi]

Subsequently, God restated that he would care for Abram and his descendants. In reply, Abram pointed out that this assurance appeared unlikely, as Abram didn't have any children, and upon his death all his possessions would pass to his servants. God reassured Abram by making a one-sided covenant (an unbreakable promise) ensuring that he would fulfil his oath. God put Abram to sleep during the inauguration and reiterated that Abram would be the father of many nations. God also promised the geographical area traversed by Abram to Abram, but only in the fourth generation. This was because God was waiting for the self-destructive practices of the people currently living in the region to fully mature. After speculating how an unknown God could fulfill transcendent promises, Abram at the age of eighty-six, and Sarai, his barren wife aged seventy-six, had a child with Sarai's servant, Hagar, who named the boy, Ishmael. In todays' ethics, this action would probably be deemed as 'rape'.

When Abram was ninety-nine, God informed him that he was now ready to fulfil his promises and give Abram a son through Sarai. God then ordained circumcision for males and told Abram (whose name means 'exalted father') to keep his faith alive by changing his name to Abraham (father of multitudes) and the name of Sarai (princess) to Sarah (woman of strength). This action was to reflect and remind them of God's Word.

Some years after the birth of this miraculous son, named Isaac, God required Abraham to physically sacrifice this God-given child. Despite the promise made by God to Abram/Abraham, regarding the future of this son, Abraham demonstrated considerable lack of faith in reacting to God's sacrificial plan, when he said in effect, 'Um, excuse me! Rather than kill my only miraculously given son, can't you just use Ishmael instead?' God responded in effect, 'No. Don't panic. I also have uses for him.' And in accordance with his assertion, from Ishmael came twelve tribes who eventually became the Arab and Muslim people. Abraham went on to obey God, regarding God's instruction, fully convinced that, if necessary, God would raise Isaac from the dead.[xvii]

After Abraham, a complete history of God's hand-picked family can be read. Starting in the Old Testament with Abraham's son Isaac (born to Sarah, as God promised), Isaac sired two sons, Esau and Jacob. Now, Jacob, whom God later renamed Israel, sired twelve sons who became the heads of the twelve tribes of Israel. Preceding this, however, there was a famine in Canaan where Jacob resided, which led him to question his sons, saying words to the effect, 'Why are you just sitting looking at each other? Get down to Egypt where they have food and buy some for us!' This was the first step for the forebears of the future nation of Israel moving to Egypt, commencing as a group of seventy-five individuals whose numbers increased with the passing of time. When their population had multiplied to the point of apparently becoming a threat to Egypt's security, they were enslaved by the Egyptians. (The book of Numbers records around 600,000 fighting men soon after they escaped Egypt hundreds of years later.)[xviii]

Morality

That God is a God of morals is clearly shown in these early Jewish patriarchal accounts, which can be perused between the biblical books of Exodus to Judges. They are replete with lessons of good and bad morality, obedience and disobedience, faithfulness, reliance, trust, strength of character, determination, faith, aggression, error, contrivance, deceit, and wisdom. These accounts reveal God's attitude and reactions to human struggles, as well as his regard of sin and disobedience. In fact, God-imposed morals are the crucial requirements for healthy living to suture and stabilise the building blocks of civilized societies. Where few ethical values with questionable moral integrity exist, there is no peaceful society, only dissension between people, families, and communities. Strong morality produces relative peace and prosperity. There is a reason for this!

God made humans and issued them a set of morals for what is known in the motoring world as 'best running conditions.' Doing absolutely nothing for personal salvation or redemption, these instructions merely serve as a vital measure to lay out what God expects from, and advises his family to follow, to enhance life.[xix] A vital and perfect guideline! In similar fashion a father might instruct his infant son by saying, 'Keep your eyes on me and do what I tell you' – the reason being to maintain focus on learning how to walk. God provided ten absolutes; imperative moral laws for continuous and successful living.[xx]

1. Make sure God is your most intimate companion and lawgiver: -
2. Take care not to allow anyone or anything to supersede the relationship between you and God: -
3. Never do anything wrong or questionable and try to rationalise it as 'condoned by God'. There will be consequences![xxi]:-
4. Keep God's instructions as your everyday focus and concentrate on helping others: -
5. Take special pains to honour your parents: -
6. Don't murder: -
7. Don't touch another person's spouse: -
8. Don't pilfer or steal: -
9. Never denigrate or lie about another person: - and
10. Don't yearn after something or someone belonging to another person.[xxii]

Taken from the Holy Bible, these constitute the solid pillars for building a successful personal and social existence. Secondary morals that govern the quality of integrity of personal life are found in the first five books of the Bible: in the book of Proverbs, in the teachings of Jesus Christ, and spread throughout the Bible. God's teachings all combine for a perfect and peaceful personal existence on earth.

A brief sample follows:

- Forgive all people always.[xxiii]
- Living life according to your own dictates will eventually lead to your permanent demise.[xxiv]
- Let mercy and truth be your guiding axioms.[xxv]
- Ensure God is paramount in your life and treat others as you would like to be treated.[xxvi]

God emphasises, through the prophet Hosea, that the first ten principles, mentioned above, describes the method he used to teach Israel to walk upright and justly. They were never designed as a 'Law' for national government so much as personal commandments to compare one's own conduct against God's requirements. However, the priesthood made it into an inflexible set of rules which Jesus dismantled in Mat. 23:1-36. Additionally, it was never presented to the individual as such. Only King David appears to have regarded it as personal.

Resultingly, God scorned their integrity after the repeated distraction of selfishness, immorality, and idolatry caused them to fall into destructive ways. The Jewish history demonstrates they never had any intention of conforming to God's instruction, but how they were determined to minimally follow God's precepts while focusing on their own aspirations.

God's instruction was to ensure that his hearers did well on all occasions. Humankind has been granted free-will, allowing the choice to follow or spurn God's instructed living conditions. Unfortunately, over time, nearly all humanity has jettisoned or modified most biblical morals to favour personal expediency, which short-sightedly responds to the question, 'What's most profitable for me right now?' Some basic morals are still intrinsically self-evident but are easily manipulated to suit the occasion. In fact, most of the imperative ten instructions are lightly esteemed in many places around the world! Global societies resultingly suffer unbelievable horrors! C. S. Lewis, (a famed Christian writer of the 20th Century) in his book *Mere Christianity*, explains the reason for this resulting mistreatment of human dignity under the heading, 'The Law of Human Nature':

> **"He** [Man] **cannot disobey those laws which he shares with other things** [physical laws]; **but the law which is peculiar to his human nature, the law he does not share with animals or vegetables or inorganic things, is the one he can disobey if he chooses** [moral law]."[xxvii]

Apart from the laws of physics, freedom of moral choice exists for man alone, but disregarding God's moral law leads to misery for people.

So how do God's moral laws affect us in our immediate environment? Man is held accountable for the moral issues God has revealed to us. Of this we are reminded in the book of Deuteronomy, especially. Things of God not shown to us are none of our concern because they apply to every living thing that is subject to the physical laws of nature; However, man is ultimately held responsible regarding God's moral issues. God's assessment of Israel's casual disregard of his moral axioms is revealed in Isaiah 28. Here God metaphorically describes the result of Israel's trying to manage their own circumstances within their human inadequacies *(Isa. 28:20 NKJV):*

> **"For the bed is too short to stretch out** *on,* **and the covering so narrow that one cannot wrap himself** *in it.* **"**

Somehow, when directed along selfish lines, one's life is never quite as comfortable or satisfying as one wishes. Having fought and struggled to arrive at a certain point, incredibly, it feels insufficient, and a new struggle commences to get somewhere else. Then the whole cycle is repeated. Not even wealthy people can escape these troubling times.

A Separated Group

God renamed Jacob as Israel, and long after Jacob's passing, God named Jacob's burgeoning descendants as the nation of Israel. After hundreds of years Israel had become enslaved to the Egyptians who were alarmed at Israel's growing potential. But amazingly, God deliberately chose Israel from all the nations. Deuteronomy 10:15 (NLT) records,

> **"Yet the Lord chose your ancestors as the objects of his love, and he chose you, their descendants, above all other nations, as is evident today."**

We begin to examine Israel in Egypt, starting in the book of Exodus, and their growth to becoming a large population. Including the attitudes and errors of group thinking and action, and individuals who stood against the crowd. Also, the deliverance from slavery, the supernatural preservation of an unwilling people, heroes who refused to acknowledge natural weakness over God's promises, supernatural deliverance from enemies, and much more.

Required to institute the Feast of Passover as a condition to Israel's rescue from slavery in Egypt, this was symbolically prophetic pointing to the crucifixion of Jesus Christ, God's son, centuries later. This crucial step was and is an essential and critical part of redemption and longevity, originally for the Jewish nation, and for the Christian now. The provision of the Passover demonstrated that without the shedding of blood there can be no forgiveness of sin or redeeming salvation. Unless we avail ourselves of God's rescuing provision, which is salvation through the shed blood of

Jesus Christ, we will remain enslaved to selfish, self-serving actions that will finally precipitate humanity's demise. It is Christ's innocently spilt blood that procures salvation.

Interestingly, God's original promise to Abraham was that he would bless those who blessed Abraham and curse those who cursed Abraham. When God released Israel from Egypt and they were journeying to God's Promised Land, they were aggressively confronted and opposed by the nations of Amalek, Midian, and Moab. In accordance with God's promise to Abraham that 'whoever curses you I will curse,' over time the nations of Amalek, Midian, and Moab have disappeared from the face of the earth. The Canaanite, Amorite, Hittite, Perizzite, Hivite, and Jebusite peoples inhabiting the land offended God by their idolatries and immoral practices and were earmarked by God for destruction as nations by Israel, with the proviso that Israel must destroy these people, or else they would be used to plague Israel with the same afflictions God had planned for those peoples. God *hates* sin and will not condone it!

A perusal of Israel's history confirms that in the wake of Israel's casual treatment of God's instruction, this is exactly what happened. Israel was oppressed for scores of years, by the very people they had failed to obliterate. They spent many years subservient to the people they were directed to destroy. As recognition of God's imperatives faded, Israel sacrificed God's planned reality of his presence for mere religious belief; thus, expediency replaced moral definition.

It would be advantageous, at this point, to highlight God's intention toward Israel.

Of all the nations of the world, which God owned, Exodus 19 informs us how God said, in effect, 'You will have noticed what I did to Egypt (your former oppressor), and how I brought you miraculously to myself. If you hold to my requirements, I will make you a very special nation of priests – (rather like a young man proposing marriage to a young female).

It was around here in the time of Moses that God introduced himself to humanity. God spoke face-to-face with Moses, instructing him to deliver Israel from Egypt. Exodus 34 records God giving his name as 'YHVH' (pronounced like the action of breathing) and describing his personal attributes: A God who is compassionate, gracious, slow to anger, abounding in love and faithfulness, maintaining love, forgiving wickedness, rebellion and sin. Yet not leaving the unrepentant unpunished even down to the fourth generation.[xxviii]

God also went on to describe his intention for Israel in chapter 34 verses 10-15; God intended to move ahead of the nation and to perform spectacular miracles on Israel's behalf. The condition was only that they made a point of obeying God precisely, to avoid social contact with the current inhabitants, and to avoid making any agreements with these people. Additionally, they were to destroy all so-called gods and the implements of worship of these people.

All of this, Moses was required to explain to the nation of Israel. He was also to establish the Priesthood as God's defining representation of his purposes.

Chapter 24 reveals how the Israelite nation wholeheartedly agreed and accepted these requirements, probably looking forward to these miraculous outworkings, in spite of their terror at the display of God's power.

Thus, the covenant was ratified.

As mentioned above, the validity of these promises rested on the implementation of shed blood, as demonstrated a few months before when the condition for delivering Israelite lives rested on the smeared sacrificial blood on the door frames of their houses. In similar fashion, God established the priesthood on the shedding of sacrificial blood, which must occur unceasingly. This process is extensively covered through the books of Exodus, Leviticus and Deuteronomy.

The comprehension of sacrificial blood enhancing the validity of the Covenant was demonstrated throughout the Old Testament. Even when Israel wondered far off the prescribed terms of the Covenant, God honoured his part by respecting the blood sacrifices for the duration of Israelite history. As God explained to Moses, in Exodus 34, he forgives all confessed sin – until the shed sacrificial blood is spurned.

However, Israel had limited response – even in the face of their miraculous deliverance from Egypt. Quite possibly, in their former thinking, in Egypt they had at least personally owned something, however harsh, whereas in their current visible evaluation, all they had now was sand! The wealth of Egypt, of which they had become possessors, seemingly escaped their notice. They made issue that they had nothing to eat, yet they carried away the spoils of Egypt, including their own livestock[xxix]. Perhaps this was just a protest against having to walk, live, and exist in a desert, having no evidence of personal selfish achievements to distract them from their perceived poverty and displacement. On the other hand, they grasped the significance of blood sacrifice.

It might be said that it was a simple case of, 'better the devil you know than the God you don't understand.' Transcendent promises from a faceless, heavenly God did not appear to be a worthwhile alternative. Perhaps this tension is best captured by the challenge of the Prophet Elijah, *"How much longer will you waver, hobbling between two opinions?"*[xxx]

History reveals that Israel never had any intention of conforming to God's plan of intimate fellowship. (In fact, Amos chapter three reveals how Israel was the only nation God had ever treated with unrequited intimacy.) Their choices demonstrated their preference to conform their world view according to the surrounding nation's practices. On the other hand, they did maintain animal sacrifice throughout their history, which God honoured, in spite of their other faulty practices. Their actions revealed they wanted God to honour his promise of supernatural deliverance, but they didn't want to actually do anything to receive it. They merely wanted God to honour his prescribed part without them having to pay their dues. However, even so, God sent relief on a number of occasions.

The Book of Judges records many unethical events in Israel's history. These include leadership squabbling, a man sacrificing his daughter on the whim of a foolish vow, constructing personal 'gods' etc., as well as subscribing to the values and practices of the false-god ideology of surrounding nations, all of which became the norm for Israel.

It would be pertinent, at this point, to note the many times, recorded in The Old Testament, how God spoke to direct Israel's thinking and responses in order to form them into his righteous, intimate people.

Isa 1:3 Even an ox knows its owner, and a donkey recognises its master's care – but Israel doesn't know its master. My people don't recognize my care for them.

Jer 2:2 This is what the Lord says: "I remember how eager you were to please me as a young bride long ago...

Jer 2:3 In those days Israel was holy to the Lord, the first of his children..."

Lam 2:14 Your prophets have said so many foolish things, false to the core.

Lam 3:2 The faithful love of the Lord never ends. His mercies never cease.

Hos 1:2 This will illustrate how Israel has acted like a prostitute by turning against the Lord and worshiping other gods. (All from NLT)

This represents a very tiny portion in God's constant urging for Israel to return to God.

God constantly instructed Israel to lay aside their concepts of retributive deity, gleaned from Egypt and surrounding nations. Examining, amongst other entities, the origins of human invention of deity, it can be seen that the Egyptians worshiped cattle. Thus, when Moses was delayed in bringing down the stone tablets of God's moral laws, it was not surprising that a golden calf, of all possible entities, apparently just amazingly appeared in the fires of Mount Sinai.[xxxi] That a god should resemble a cow was already established in the psyche of the people!

Quite probably, cow worship evolved through the practices of the surrounding nations. They had made an image of a bull's head with a human body, called Molech, to whom they sacrificed not only offerings, but also their own children. Although not yet physically established by archaeological means, the book of Leviticus chapter 18, especially, deals with this whole practice, and God's attitude to the detestable concept of this god.

However, God continued to uphold his planned promise to Abraham regarding keeping Abraham's descendants with special consideration.

As mentioned above, today the nations of Amalek, Midian, Moab, or any of the original inhabitants of that region no longer exist. God may move very slowly, but he is very thorough. Other than Egypt, which originally gave Jacob succour, however meagrely, no other nation on earth has retained their original configuration or name. Only Egypt and Israel exist in their original identities. It is notable that while the people of Israel have yet to fully learn their lesson and were consequently scattered all over the globe for nearly two thousand years, they retained their identity and religious practices wherever they were found. Today, after thousands of years, as promised by God so long ago, they are largely back in their original land. The Jewish nation remains intact and is living in a land still called Israel. They are God's chosen people in God's chosen land. God has honoured his promises.

Once God has spoken, it can be readily gleaned from these recorded accounts, that regardless of the passage of time, and whatever occurs, his declared word will happen!

The biblical book of Hosea provides a fascinating record from God's perspective of the life of Israel and his promise of their eventual redemption. Apart from that record, the book of Judges is a forensic account of Israel wandering off God's ordained path: falling into murderous situations, desperately appealing to God for help, receiving someone to rescue them, and then repeating the same depressing cycle. Following that, rather than listen attentively and continuously to God's instructions, after many years, they demanded a king so they could emulate the surrounding nations. God reluctantly granted their demand, and they were consequently ruled by many bad and a few reasonable kings. God sent several prophets with the intention of correcting their meanderings. God revealed his response to their wayward thinking in Hosea 13:11 (NLT):

"In my anger I gave you kings, and in my fury, I took them away."

Knowing that sinful man has a proclivity toward selfish accumulation, and manipulative tendencies, God sought to spare Israel from unreasonable human dictates and deal with them directly. However, as was demonstrated at Sinai many years before, God's direct intervention was never going to happen. On that occasion all the tangible glory, majesty and awesome splendour of God's presence was on display,[xxxii] but this merely re-enforced Israel's preconceived understanding of the deities they had heard from surrounding nations: that the gods were terribly fierce, demanding, and manifestly unfair!

To begin with, God was prepared to continue with his original intention of going into the promised land ahead of God's intentions for Israel. However, having reached the gateway to the promised land, Israel would not accept God's word concerning his original miraculous plan for Israel. They wailed in despair, determined not to believe God. As a result, God relegated them to wander around the wilderness until they died, forty years later. He determined to use their children instead.

Even though the children responded to God in similar manner as their parents had, God commenced his intention of supernatural intervention on Israel's behalf. The walls of Jericho miraculously collapsed when Israel obeyed instruction. But rather than generating great faith, sin and error started to unravel immediately as disobedience reared its ugly head. Greed and selfishness manifested as a man, named Achan directly ignored God's instruction and helped himself to forbidden property.

From there, they disobeyed instruction to annihilate various nations; they made agreements with nations they were instructed to annihilate, and more. As a result, Israel suffered disaster after disaster. Yet, even after their failures, when the heart of one of the kings appeared contrite toward God, he supernaturally destroyed 185,000 of the enemy troops in one night. Additionally, this is probably also because after allowing the relative king of Assyria to conquer northern Israel, this king attempted to overcome Jerusalem, which was in Judea and not given to Assyria. This effectively removed Assyria from any future aspirations.

Finally, Israel was invaded by the Babylonian army and taken captive to Babylon for about seventy years. This was at God's direction in response to Israel ignoring God's original instruction with repeated warnings regarding Sabbath-keeping. Much of the Old Testament outlines this tragic event of Israel in captivity. This is recorded most spectacularly in the book of Jeremiah, who is commonly known as the 'weeping prophet'. This description is due to the experiences he endured, and the unfavourable messages God impressed upon him to deliver over his lifespan. (This event of captivity reflects an expression of God's heart and methods regarding disobedient children, even allowing God's favoured people to be taken captive by adverse forces). But, as a result, Israel never again defaulted on God's commands regarding Sabbath-keeping; there-after taking attentive pains to acknowledge God's requirements and earnestly looking forward to God's promise of sending a saviour to rescue them from their subjugation to various nations.

God frequently sent prophets to inform the people of the coming saviour/rescuer, including his plan for the final days of Messianic rule. Some prophets also delivered personal messages to individuals, usually of rescue, healing, or judgement. In fact, the prophet Amos described, in chapter three, how God does nothing unless he first informs his prophets. Following about seven hundred years of God's fruitless pleading with Israel, the prophet Zechariah was sent to Israel to demonstrate that God was no longer going to uphold his original agreement with Israel. He announced how the three shepherds, namely the prophets, the priests, and the leaders were responsible for obscuring the true conditions of the covenant. He physically broke two staves to visibly demonstrate that the agreement was now broken and cancelled. He also noted that the people were completely cognisant of the implication of this action.

Prior to this, the prophet Jeremiah declared how God intended to establish a new covenant, completely different to the current covenant, or Testament, and Isaiah chapter 31 reveals the introduction of the Holy Spirit to galvanise the working of this new covenant.

From the action of Zechariah, for about four hundred years God ceased speaking through the prophets,[xxxiii] and in this famine of God's Word, the people of Israel searched for God's encouragement looking to religiously revered groups of people, such as the Pharisees and the Essenes. The Essenes were a monastic, cave-dwelling society that focused on the true essence of the Law of Moses, and generally avoided contact with other people. Interpretation of the Word of God had fallen largely into the hands of the Sadducees and the Pharisees by the time of the New Testament.[xxxiv]

The Sadducees were secular aristocrats with minimal transcendent values, but who directed political and religious issues, and the Pharisees interpreted scripture and conveyed their own understanding to the people. Both groups seized God's yardstick for successful living, turning it into complicated mandatory law, adding their own harsh, personal interpretations, which Jesus later criticized by pointing out how, over time, God's morals had been substituted with self-indulgent, man-made drivel.

The Issues of God on Earth

These leaders of Israel were totally engrossed in their own interpretations and expectations of retributive deity, based on their collective worldview. Therefore, when Jesus Christ, God's predicted Messiah, rode into Jerusalem on a donkey, as prescribed by scripture, and despite his numerous demonstrated miracles and the confounding wisdom he showed, he was not recognized but was rejected as a fraud and heretic!

It is perhaps possible that the interpreters of Jewish scripture perceived two redeemers in the writings of the prophets: a suffering Messiah and also a victorious, conquering Messiah. However, Jesus didn't match either of their expectations. He didn't appear transcendently from nowhere as a gift from God or lead on an all-conquering army. The nation of Israel eagerly anticipated that someone would arise who would permanently relieve their political subjugation from Rome and the occupation of mere men, who had been their master's for some time. They supposed this would enable them to resume their former God-favoured pathway through life.

This common expectation is shown in Acts chapter 1 when the disciples asked the newly risen Christ if he intended to restore the kingdom to Israel, at that time. Israel wanted the benefits of God's favour, but without fulfilling their part of the agreement. (It's almost amusing to read how the Pharisees, in their self-evaluation, vehemently denied ever being enslaved to any man, conveniently ignoring, enslavement, invasion, occupation, and death under Egypt, Assyria, Babylon, Medes and Persians, Greece, and their current Roman masters!) In their own estimation, they were flawless, immovable, and untouchable. They were merely enduring an unjust occupation.

The complete Jewish history was one of vacillating between the fearful reality of God's presence and the apparent appeal of foreign deities. They wanted to believe God was all for their welfare, quite prepared to pay obeisance to a higher power, but rather than rest in complete trust in God's leadership, they belligerently preferred to evaluate their current circumstances as being deprived and needy. They were interested only in ameliorating their own immediately perceived issues.

And yet, as he does to ours, God pandered to their feebleness. To Israel, enlightened expediency, based on observable experience, seemed of superior value when compared with faith and obedience.

The Consequences of Choice

God warned the people of Israel, Deuteronomy reveals, that their persistent, vacillating inclinations and actions would remove them from God's Promised Land to slavery under malevolent rulers in foreign countries. Here they would be seduced to admire and cherish objects made by man's hand and come to regard these objects/idols as being the ones responsible for deliverance from hard times! This being the case, selected tangible choices would obviously supersede transcendent possibilities! Furthermore, they would surmise that should this fictitious deliverance method fail, it would be because some higher deity was meddling with them for entertainment,[xxxv] not because they were personally wrong. This attitude sums up the essence of a false god. In other words, Israel would consider that their attitude would be 'good things happen because the gods smile on us; bad things happen at the gods' petulant and inexplicable whims.'

The book of Jeremiah records how some women concluded that after they ceased burning incense to the Queen of Heaven (a pagan goddess), they perceived how they had become plagued by war and famine. Therefore, in their understanding, in order to ensure protection, they should return to burning incense to the 'Queen of heaven'. Apparently, their idea of a true God was for him to keep them warm and snuggly regardless of their actions and attitudes.

And so, the universal characterisation of deity that we now recognise from ancient mythology, for example, persuaded everyone to understand that the gods must be appeased lest they maliciously single you out for brutal amusement. This was the Israelite evaluation of the Jewish God too! Even the book of Job records how God saw Job as an upright and upstanding man, yet Job, in his book, chapter one, sacrificed to God on behalf of his children just in case they had done something that unwittingly offended

God! In a sense Job was 'pre-paying anticipated penalties' to the God he thought he knew, hoping to ward off any retributive action. His motive was like someone voluntarily pre-submitting payments to ameliorate any demands made by heavenly extortion. When Job realised his error, it is recorded at the end of his book he said, 'I had only heard about you before (via other people's ideas), but now I have seen (appreciated) you with my own eyes.'

This traditionally erroneous evaluation of God's character had pervaded multiple generations of Israelite beliefs, and this was clearly displayed by Phillip, one of Jesus' own disciples, in John chapter 14. The gospel of John 14:5-7 firstly records the disciple Thomas' uncertainty regarding God's character as being identical to Jesus'. And then John 14:8, records the disciple Philip, obviously mystified by his observance of Jesus' speech and actions, but who also claimed to be equal to God, asked Jesus that the Father be revealed. Presumably this was so that Phillip could contrast Jesus' demeanour with the ubiquitously accepted religious understanding of God. Phillip couldn't grasp how the apparently 'harsh' God of Israelite scriptural history could also be the inexplicably kind and loving person of Jesus Christ. In John 14: 9 (NLT) Jesus said,

> **"Have I been with you all this time...yet you still don't know who I am? Anyone who has seen me has seen the Father".**

Israel had continued to ignore God's spoken directives regarding morality, intimacy, and listening to God for guidance and God's patience with Israel started to wear thin.

Jesus declared the conclusion of the Old Testament by describing John the Baptist as the greatest born to man but the least in the kingdom of heaven – possibly showing the difference between the natural human of the Old Testament and the spiritually reborn human of the New Testament. Jesus proclaimed that he had come to finalise and complete the Law of Moses and the prophets and commence a new creation based on the shedding of his innocent blood and personal faith.

This point in time and the narrative demands a contrast between the 'fearful, harsh God of the Old Testament' and the almost 'hippie' Christ of the New Testament. The fact is they both display the same character because they are the same God. The first time God declared his character to Moses as compassionate, gracious, slow to anger, abounding in love and faithfulness, maintaining love to thousands, forgiving wickedness rebellion and sin, yet punishing the unrepentant. (NIV)

Jesus Christ came as a visible demonstration of that same character. This is clearly seen through the amazing miracles he performed for a collection of apparent 'nobodies'; through his teaching; through his attitude and demeanour; through his actions to blatant error; to his reactions to unjust treatment levelled toward himself; to his willingness to enlarge on moral concepts – and much more.

The God of the Old Testament revealed himself with an unnatural display of power and authority, announcing how he planned to go ahead of the nation of Israel to supernaturally displace the offensive nations currently usurping the land he had earmarked for his special people. In demonstration he supernaturally levelled the walls of Jericho, after bringing them out of Egypt, giving them food out of nowhere, giving them water from a rock, and on and on.

Jesus came from the opposite tack. He was born as a nobody, gentle to all (except moral thieves and blatant evil), displaying kindness in the face of aggression.

The God of the Old Testament inspired fear and resentment. The Jesus of the New Testament demonstrated how to live within the pleasure and respect of the God of the Old Testament.

End of the Line

As a result, after God's chastening them regularly through numerous oppressive events (to reverse their adopted worldview),[xxxvi] and after his warning them of his disciplinary intentions, 'I will no longer have pity on the people of the land...I will let them fall into the hands of each other... and I will not rescue them', God announced his intention to withdraw from his original covenant. This passage also predicts Jesus' betrayal for the price of a slave[xxxvii].

In a unique display of immense, transcendent emotional grief and disappointment, Jesus stood within the precincts of the Temple, recorded in Mat. 23, and revealed how he had always yearned to gather his people close together with him (much like a mother hen gathers her chickens under her wings for protection, warmth, and intimate instruction). But the Jews had always rebelled against the concept of attentive compliance, preferring rather to follow their own lifestyle, while expecting and pleading with God to rescue them in their resulting self-generated disasters. The book of Judges, especially, is replete with examples. They preferred to live on their own selected terms and only sought God's intervention when things went awry. Jesus later emotionally pronounced judgement on the nation by declaring that their domicile and heritage would be abandoned and left to them as desolate.[xxxviii]

This above abrogation was confirmed by the High Priest when Jesus was brought before the High Priest. Jesus prophesied that he is the Christ, and this would be clearly revealed and confirmed by his return to earth in the clouds. In a resulting fit of rage, the High Priest tore his priestly garment. This was customarily done by ripping open the collar, and as he was due to administer the sacrifice later that same day, he would therefore probably have been robed in priestly garments of High Priest. It is interesting that the construction the High Priest's

Ephod (chest-covering) contained twelve precious stones representing all the tribes of Israel,[xxxix] and symbolically signifying that it was the high priest's intension to rip Israel from this blasphemous notion that Jesus was the Christ.

Now, according to the law given by God to Moses, the robe of the priestly garment was never to be torn![xl] Seemingly, in response to the High Priest's disregard of God's instruction, scripture records that when Jesus died on the cross, the curtain in the temple between the Holy Place and the Holy of Holies was ripped from top to bottom. This unwittingly signified the termination of the Jewish legal system,[xli] simultaneously opening the door for all to access God's presence. In a sense, the action of the High Priest, dressed in robes representing the nation of Israel, spurned the integrity of God's covenant, and so foolishly endorsed God's cancelled agreement with Israel. To quote the similarly relevant words of the prophet Samuel to Israel's King Saul, in 1 Samuel 15:23 – **"because you have rejected the Word of the Lord, he has rejected you as king"**. (NIV)

The High Priest sealed the deal.

On the cross Jesus said, 'It is finished!' The old covenant was completed. His innocent Blood became the catalyst of the New Covenant, which was instigated at Christ's death.[xlii]

From here, the Jewish comprehension of God's intention was put into a stupor, or sleep.[xliii]

It can be seen, looking through Wikipedia and historical accounts, how Jewish/Roman wars and struggles occurred between sixty-six CE and one hundred and thirty-five CE. As Jesus prophesied and as God had warned in Deuteronomy chapter twenty-eight, ultimately the Jews were forcibly spread throughout the world. In CE seventy the Romans destroyed the Temple and began the global disbursement of the Jews.

The New Direction

Jesus had introduced many radically different ideas about God and the reality of God's attitude towards humanity. These ideas were totally estranged to prior human understanding.

> Love your enemies and pray for them: -
> First seek God, and everything else will be added to you: -
> Whoever does the Father's will is my brother, sister and mother: -
> I am the way and the truth and the life. No one comes to the Father except through me: -
> Forgive, and you'll be forgiven. Don't forgive, and you will find yourself in a prison of torture:
> Humility trumps superiority: -
> I'm the resurrection and the life. Whoever believes in me will live, even if he dies. -
> And many others!

But Jesus also introduced a way of thought that took even his own disciples by total surprise: Some women came to see Jesus, records Mark 10:13-16, bringing their small children with them. The disciples were staunch believers in the commonly accepted patriarchy and started to warn off the women and children. Their attitude made Jesus angry, and he rebuked his disciples, saying the kingdom of heaven requires gentle acceptance and the innocent expectation of children. If they didn't adopt this attitude, they themselves would never be received by God. There is no Biblical record that this evaluation had ever entered Israel's erstwhile thinking.

Jesus also contradicted the accepted teachings of the perceived black and white harshness of the Old Testament Law by presenting it as actually being relevant (similar to upgrading a monochrome computer monitor into a monitor with a colour screen.) For example, Mark chapter ten deals with the divorce question. Jesus brought out how divorce was conceded as a concession, but as it involves adultery, God never intended this to be.

The Old Testament provides a glimpse into the engine room of God's plan for humanity, whereas the New Testament highlights the limitations, clarification, and limited specification regarding salvation, in the Old Testament morals/Law. It also expands on attitudes, behaviour, and relationship and actions toward people. These conditions appear unemphasised in the Law, but are clarified in the New Testament

Over centuries Jesus' new ideas evolved into the moral and legal backbone of Western civilization; especially in relation to the legal presumption of innocence as prescribed in the drafting of the Magna Carta. This foundational document recognized the basic values of the individual: men, women, and children. There is no equivalent found in any other major civil or religious society. The gentle peace and appeal of this amazing reward to life draws all eastern countries too. The problem arises because immigrants often want to drag their evil religious systems along with them, and God will not share his glory with anyone. The benefits of the Christian West is appealing to them – but not the intimacy. Therefore, as their fallacious ideas are accepted by foolish people within the 'Christian' country, Christian principles wane and evil ensues. If it didn't work back home, how is it going to work here? Why not just stay at home? Law and Order is part and parcel of the Christian West jurisprudence.

This is God's point of view, from Isa 2:6

For the Lord has rejected his people…because they have filled their land with practices from the East… they have made alliances with pagans, (NIV)

Now, God declared his intention and choice is that all his people would become like his Son, Jesus, who dedicated large swathes of his time in the presence of his heavenly Father. Jesus spent his remaining time teaching and instructing his disciples and ministering to the needs of the sick and needy. Jesus' life was a living example of always following the Holy Spirit's prompting to meet the ongoing hurts of sick-and-wanting people. However, in order to follow the Holy Spirit of God, there are a few hurdles to overcome in achieving this aspiration. To begin with, all men must recognise and accept they are going to exist forever, but as sinners they are therefore earmarked to die forever. So, the first step to succeed in God's plan is to:

> **"Turn from your selfish ways, take up your cross, and follow me** (Jesus)."[xliv]

There is no mysterious secret about God's plan. Jesus said:

> **"I have told you all this so that you may have peace in me. Here on earth, you will have many trials and sorrows. But take heart, because I have overcome the world."**[xlv]

Jesus revealed that God's ordained plan from the outset, was to mature us to completion through our adoption of a godly lifestyle, by imitating Jesus' example, even though it usually requires personal suffering and malevolence, contrary to our personal preferences. Quite often, with adults, acknowledgment of the presence of God comes as the result of suffering. Psalm 105:18,19 suggest suffering is the catalyst to maturity and development, instilling 'iron' in our soul. Therefore, we teach our children to worship God, in order to give them an accurate directional signpost for when they later face the experiential malevolence of maturity. Suffering proffers a choice of either turning to God for instruction or turning away from God. Choice of response is the only God-given right we have!

Christianity Begins

Jesus hand-picked twelve male disciples and revealed to them that he had come as the sacrificial lamb on behalf of humanity. Jesus confirmed this, around thirty CE, when he was crucified on the day of Passover. Jesus declared he was the reason for, and fulfilment of the original Passover instituted during the time of Moses, to shed his blood on behalf of humankind. John the Baptist acknowledged the purpose of Jesus' intent at the time of Jesus' baptism. Jesus also clarified and demonstrated how to live a life pleasing to God, and revealed how the Law of Moses had a latent implication for successful personal relationships. It was not merely symbolic of God's vital moral standards for man's success. This concept of scriptural duality, usually known as a 'Type', is perhaps more clearly explained by the following bible verses in First Corinthians, that were spoken in the context of providing material and financial support for gospel workers:

> **"For the Law of Moses says, "You must not muzzle an ox to keep it from eating as it treads out the grain." Was God thinking only about oxen when he said this? Wasn't he actually speaking to us? Yes, it was written for us, so that the one who plows and the one who threshes the grain might both expect a share of the harvest."[xlvi]**

Another notable point is how often the number 'three' appears in many Old Testament references. For example, when establishing the covenant with Abram three three-year-old animals were sacrificed; when three angels visited Abraham, three measures of meal were prepared; where Joseph interpreted dreams, three days featured prominently; Jonah was in the whale for three days and nights; a rope of three strands is not easily broken, and many others. In fact, Jesus went on to prophesy, referring to the Jonah account, that in similar pattern to Jonah, so he too would rise on the third day after his crucifixion. This he did! Jesus also reassured his followers, at that time, that he would return to collect them.

While talking about 'threes' it should be pointed out how our complete bodies consist of Body, Soul, and Spirit. Body is the container in which we live. Soul refers to the thoughts, intentions, mind, and emotions (to some extent), and Spirit, which is the driving force of our existence as well as the means of communication with God.

The Godhead too is made up of Father, Son, and Holy Spirit.

One becomes a Christian by recognizing and identifying with the risen Christ and vocally espousing his resurrection and Lordship. A person's lifestyle will begin to change once awakened to eternal reality. Things that seemed important in one's life somehow lose their attraction and influence as new spiritual values and interests grow. At this point in time, it is imperative to maintain fellowship with other Christians for encouragement, focus, consistency, and growth. Affiliation alone with a church or religious group does nothing regarding salvation. Mere Identification with various faiths around the world supplies and achieves nothing except, perhaps, a feeling of self-righteousness. However, their conscience will still condemn each person! Mankind's arranged and prescribed religious actions are also worthless, as noted in the following scripture:

> **"These** [religious] **rules may seem wise because they require strong devotion, pious self-denial, and severe bodily discipline. But they provide no help in conquering a person's evil desires."**[xlvii]

Without the continuous working of the Holy Spirit manifesting the reality of Christ's presence in our lives, everything else is merely a religious facade.

Christianity emerged on the day the Holy Spirit was revealed on earth in a new way. Three thousand people died when God's moral law was originally given to Israel after their rescue from Egypt. But when the Holy Spirit physically entered man's domain, three thousand people were born again into the church at Pentecost. This contrasts the vast difference of accepting Christianity over identification with Jewish law: life versus death![xlviii] Jesus declared that the only way to eternal life was, in practice, to abandon one's self-centred personal drive, acknowledge the risen Christ as one's sole decision-maker, and seek God's direction. In other words, become a new creation in Christ by turning away from wanton error, and paying attention to the Holy Spirit's guiding through the conscience, thereby developing a relationship with God. The Jews had become fastidious about the physical observance of prescribed feasts and rules, but Jesus came to embody the reason behind the Covenant's symbolism and, additionally, to nail the culpability of human failure to the cross.

To further explain: the Jews were (and largely remain) focused on maintaining the physical aspects of the 'letter of the Law', whereas Jesus came to reveal the Spirit of the law: the underlying reality and intended purpose behind all prescribed laws and feasts. The Law, in itself, was never designed to enable mankind to live eternally, because the Law demands perfection, and no-one can achieve this. Therefore, through the law, no man has the remotest possibility of qualifying for redemption. However, Jesus, as God's rescuer of mankind, was the only one ever to qualify, and came to bring life eternal by vicariously, and faultlessly, fulfilling the law and dying as an eternal sacrifice on mankind's behalf, thus creating a way of redemption for mankind. The Apostle Paul described, in 2

Corinthians chapter three, how relying on and meticulously observing the Law (as given to Moses) is, in reality, a ministry of death carved in stone, compared to the freedom from condemnation which is found in the Spirit of God (This is why Jesus was crucified on behalf of mankind – to physically embody this reality).

The Jews, including Jesus' disciples, were locked into the ubiquitously accepted idea of a God who was semi-detached from their personal lives. A demanding authoritarian. Jesus, through his sayings, actions, crucifixion, and resurrection demonstrated that he was actually God on earth. Not only did he inspire intimacy with God, as God originally envisaged with Moses, on mount Sinai, but he also demonstrated a revolutionary concept of recognizing and acknowledging a deity figure. On a number of occasions, Jesus spoke of God as 'Father', and instructed his disciples, when they enquired, to speak to God as 'Father'. No religion has ever warmly identified God as their personal Father (even the Jews were never embraced as 'sons', but as servants). Rather, some supreme deities have been acknowledged as being largely indifferent progenitors who dispense petulance, anger, and requiring instant response. These religions mostly rely on obedience and obeisance to a supposed superior figure that has requirements and ideals that certainly don't consider the health or wellbeing of their adherents.

In fact, some religions insistently demand establishing superiority over all unbelieving peoples through violence and subjugation. But the essence of Christianity is totally contrary: God is worshipped by faith, in spirit, by prayer, loyalty, and intimate compliance. The Christian receives instruction, usually through their conscience, imitating Jesus' actions – often by watching the example of other mature Christians; and by staying in close communion with the Father. Furthermore, they strive to do what is good and right in life; care for others; help the helpless; bring relief and comfort to those suffering physically or mentally; and always telling and demonstrating the way to eternal life.

True fathers actively instruct, guide, correct, help, discipline, encourage, and direct their children. This can only be totally effective if they are accepted as Father. Few children would unreservedly follow the directions of a stranger. The focus of Christianity is to help others to appreciate God's truth not to aggressively oppose those who disagree from a different point of view!

But it should be noted that God introduced himself to humankind as mercy *and* justice not merely mercy. He is the epitome of perfect balance: he is slow to anger, but his wheels of justice grind with exceeding thoroughness. So, whereas the Old Testament largely reveals his justice, the New Testament reveals his mercy.

Whatever the Jews were expecting, the gentleness, genuineness, honesty, humanity, and compassion of Jesus Christ became a stumbling block in their evaluation and expectation. The spectacular nature of his miracles was conveniently and consistently ignored by religious rulers. Jewish history shows how the Jews were imitative of their surrounding neighbours and their gods, which led them to accept similar beliefs on the character and behaviour expected of a deity. Thus, they had always largely regarded God as a retributive figure, as observable in much of the Old Testament. A God who must be appeased and obeyed, or else!

As stated above, even the disciples were confused as to the nature of God, and asked Jesus to reveal the Father to them. Jesus replied that if they had perceived Jesus in action, they had seen God. This seemed to be an oxymoron to a people steeped in the idea of an angry, demanding God as their scriptures apparently portrayed. Although the perceived inflexible messages were given by a loving God through the spirit, they were flavoured via the worldview of the prophets, Therefore, the Jews apparently perceived and portrayed God as harsh, in many ways. Thus, the universal, emotional understanding of God's scripture had been misconstrued from generation to generation.

Immediately after the arrival of the Holy Spirit, Peter, one of the disciples of Jesus, preached his first message, which convicted around three thousand Jewish men of their sin and their need to change their understanding and lifestyle. Their heartfelt conversion resulted in them believing in Jesus as the Messiah and so launched the Christian Church. This mass desertion from the Jewish faith resulted in persecution by the Jewish leadership, who sought to murder all who called themselves a believer of 'the Way', an identification of faith used by early Christian believers. It was probably some years after Jesus Christ's crucifixion that believers became known as Christians, in Antioch. The name was originally intended by Jews as a sneering slur but was adopted by Christians as a reminder of their identity and value to God.

2

A Change of Track

It was soon after the outpouring of the Holy Spirit on the first followers of Jesus at Pentecost, that God set aside working with the Jews in favour of working with the Gentiles – meaning 'outsiders' from Judaism. It appears that the Jewish understanding of God's morals was not reflective of God's intentions for the world. This was confirmed when Jesus Christ told them what to expect in their future. Namely, that God's directing hand on the Jewish nation would be withheld in favour of the Gentiles.[xlix] In confirmation of this prediction, and following the destruction of Jerusalem in 70 CE, the Jews were driven out of Israel and disbursed to all nations across the world. It appears that later, God even allowed a Muslim Mosque to be built on the Temple Mount, probably to ensure that the Jews would be unable to rebuild the temple and resume their ancient ways of worship. Hence, the possibility of the Jewish 'track' of Christianity was temporarily terminated, and the bridge to the gentile track was created. The dispensation of the Law, which commenced originally with Moses, was terminated. God will resume working with the Jews when he has fulfilled his plan for the Gentiles[l], after the Rapture (or removal of the church from this world), which will close Jesus' Church Age dispensation.

God's change of track was caused by an unlikely catalyst which is recorded in chapter six of the book of Acts, where soon after the spectacular launch of the Christian Church, a dispute arose involving the distribution of food supplies amongst the widows of Jewish and

Greek believers. The normal custom of migrant Jews was to return to their birthplace to be buried following their expected death, leaving the foreign widow (and children) to fend for themselves. As Dr. R. C. Sproul (American Theologist) puts it thus.

> 'So, the pain of widowhood brings a unique dimension of loneliness. ... The widow was usually the most vulnerable and helpless person in the community. Widows had little or no means of support in ancient societies.'[li]

Adhering to the values of Jesus Christ, which were largely strange concepts to the world in general but were foreshadowed by instruction in the Jewish Old Testament,[lii] the church began looking after all the widows of the new believer community. However, Jewish believers saw themselves as superior to mere Greek believers (as instructed in the Jewish Law) and unfair prejudice in the food distribution favoured Jewish widows over widows of other nationalities. Consequently, the general excitement of the radical new lifestyle soured. This resulted in discontentment among believers, exposing racial bias. At this time, the Apostles wisely chose to 'keep the main thing the main thing' by devoting themselves to the Word of God and directed other mature believers to address the management of the new church.

There is no record of the nationality of the original seven helping believers/deacons who were elected to organise this distribution task, but their names suggest they were not of Jewish origin. One of them, Nicolas, is specifically mentioned as a convert from Antioch and therefore would probably have been of Greek origin. Stephen, one of the deacons and the first Christian martyr, spoke to the resident Jews, mentioning 'our father Abraham.' After being malevolently accused by false witnesses, he went on to recount the history of Israel, highlighting God's directing hand in their existence. He then showed how Israel's attitude was contrary to God's intentions and plan. However, instead of arousing conviction, as the apostle Peter had done, he merely provoked anger from the non-Christian Jews. Possibly, the Jews resented being confronted by a half-foreigner who took the liberty of identifying himself as a descendent of Abraham, as well as highlighting the Jews' error. In a great rage, the Jewish mob stoned Stephen to death. The backlash resulting from this murderous act released a vicious persecution against the church. Consequently, many new believers were scattered into the countryside, spreading the good news of salvation as they went.

This event, which drove Christians away from Jerusalem, constitutes the first step of the 'train' of Christianity splitting away from the hitherto purely Jewish track, to focus on Gentile inclusion. This Jewish–Gentile friction in the running of the newly formed church revealed the path of God's hand moving visibly from dealing exclusively with the Jews to collaborating more prominently with the Gentiles. Thus, from this time on, the Jewish flavour of the original church dwindled.

It wasn't immediately quite that simple, of course. For a while, the Jewish element of the new-found revelation of deliverance tried to retain the dominance of Jewish law over Christianity—the Jewish point of view supported by the apostle Peter, and the Gentile point of view supported by the apostle Paul. It became a heated issue at one documented point in the birthing stages. Acts chapter 15 records that when the apostle Paul and company had returned from one of their missionary journeys, they arrived at Antioch and clashed head-on with a Jewish contingent who maintained Jewish circumcision was imperative for salvation. Paul openly and vocally challenged Peter for his hypocritical vacillation in deferring to insistent Jewish identity at this time, after openly identifying with the gentiles prior to the Jewish contingent arriving.

Leading up to this moment, however, God completed his original plan of giving Peter the 'keys to the kingdom of God' by allowing Peter to introduce the release of the Holy Spirit to the Jews in Jerusalem at the time of Pentecost, and later to the Gentiles at Caesarea. Thus, when the freedom of the Holy Spirit amongst the Gentiles was demonstrated, acknowledged, and confirmed by the apostles and elders of the mother church, in Acts 15, the total validity of Christianity was wrested from Jewish law. The legitimacy of the Gentile church was now officially constituted, and the persecution from Jews around the Mediterranean nations intensified.

Believers spread out from living in Jerusalem with the increase of persecution, moving to Samaria and then on to the rest of the known world. This was in direct confirming response to the risen Christ's instruction in Acts chapter one. We are told that one of the original deacons, Philip ministered between Azotus and Caesarea. Caesarea was the large shipping centre of the area, from which ships travelled all over the Mediterranean, making the growing reach of the Gospel inevitable as believers scattered throughout the known world. It would seem obvious that God used Jewish persecution to spread the Gospel by dispersing the believing Christians, who happily shared their exciting faith with everyone they met, a faith encapsulated in righteousness, peace, and joy in the Holy Spirit![liii] It's the anointing of the Spirit that lifts a person to inexplicable joy and triumph, and it's the perpetual witness of the Spirit within the believer's life that maintains that joy through all situations.

It would be extremely pertinent to enlarge further on the way God shifted the emphasis of his plan to incorporate the Gentiles at the expense of the Jews. This was done largely through a man named Saul, a man born a Roman/Jew and steeped in Jewish law as a Pharisee of Pharisees, which means it can be accurately assumed that he was considered above other mere Pharisees in understanding and enactment of Jewish law. He had also studied under a man named Gamaliel, who was a renowned Pharisee and teacher.

As a young man, Saul, driven by knowledge, murder, anger, and zeal, set out, under religious authority, determined to stamp out all followers of The Way movement that worshiped and followed Jesus Christ. However, Saul had a very physical and visual encounter with Jesus Christ while on the road to Damascus. Saul was blinded and Jesus literally challenged his intentions. Suddenly realising he had been fighting against God, Saul shook with fear! All those years of studiously studying the Law came to nothing. Saul's realisation that his life had been dedicated to something altogether opposed to God's plan stunned him to the core. He was mortified, horror-struck, incredulous … and now physically blind to match his spiritual blindness.

Being helpless, he was led by the hand into the city of Damascus. For three days He did not eat or drink, demonstrating the horror and remorse he felt as he contemplated his intentions and where he had been going.

Being healed by God through the prayer of Ananias, a believer, Paul immediately converted to Christianity. Thus, as a believer Saul became not only one of the people he had set out to destroy but also the author of many of the most influential books of the New Testament, as well as being on the cutting edge of the spread of the gospel. In time, Saul became known as Paul (the apostle Paul mentioned above) and became a notable force in promoting the gospel amongst the Gentiles. But Paul's dramatic conversion and powerful subsequent influence was not without personal cost! He records in his second letter to the Corinthians the incredible times of life-sucking hardships endured during his three recorded missionary journeys undertaken around the eastern and northern countries of the Mediterranean Sea.

Paul was so focused on Jesus Christ that his whole demeanour changed virtually overnight. As much as he previously breathed hatred and murder, he now became a driven evangelist, an immovable instrument in the spread of Christianity.

As Christians moved out of the reach of Jewish persecution, fresh persecution arose from the Romans. This kept up the momentum, galvanising the surge of Christianity to go and grow. History is a living testament to the truth that Christianity thrives under pressure.

The New Testament records extraordinarily little about the continuing spread of the gospel, and from this point we must rely largely on historical and traditional Church records. Most of the book of Acts records Paul's missionary journeys through what is today Turkey, Asia Minor, Greece, and Rome. Tradition puts him in Spain as well. There is biblical record that Paul was summoned to Greece and to Rome, having been directed away from north Asia Minor, where he had been planning to go. Instead, a larger and better understanding of Christianity entered Europe in this way, obviously according to God's plan, galvanizing the unstoppable effect caused by the revolutionary ideas of Jesus Christ. The European populations became captive to a transcendent idea that resulted in forgiveness, freedom, and joy!

The Apostle Peter is recorded as being in Antioch, and tradition also puts him in Rome. The Apostle Philip is recorded in the Bible as moving through various cities before finally reaching Caesarea, where he stayed. The Apostle Thomas is reputed to have reached and preached in India. The Apostle Bartholomew apparently entered Asia Minor and the Far East. A Google computer search reveals many online accounts of the spread of the original apostles but little actual proof: tradition puts Andrew in Turkey, Matthias in Georgia, Bartholomew in India, Armenia, and Mesopotamia, and so on. While little hard evidence is available the only certainty is that Christianity spread throughout the world, as planned by God.

3

The Growth of Christianity in Europe and the Middle Ages

It is virtually impossible to accurately trace every step of the history of Christianity in Europe. We know that Paul wrote to the Christian church in Rome before his arrival there, proving that the Christian message was not quintessential to Paul, any apostle, or known person. It would have migrated to Europe by travellers, traders and soldiers who were excited to share The Good News with everybody they met. One thing is certain: the basis of Western civilization that stemmed from the influence of Christ's teachings and galvanised by the Holy Spirit, proved greater than all the opposing weapons, military force, and intentions of man. As faith and belief in the person and sayings of Jesus Christ were grasped and adopted, God's qualifying promises of 'making you the head and not the tail'[liv] by following God's directives were proved throughout Europe. European civilisation gradually rose above all other civilisations.

Since the fall of the human race, all hope of redemption had been underscored by the belief that each individual had to hopefully demonstrate their worthiness of salvation through good works. Each had to 'prove' their worthiness before God. But Jesus came and declared unheard-of concepts concerning transcendent love and kindness to humans, regardless of personal effort. And in dying to pay the penalty for our individual and collective disobedience, he released us from its bondage. Salvation did not rest on the performance of man—it was a gift free to anyone who would embrace the truth of transcendent forgiveness and love of God as a Father to child. This concept was absolutely foreign and totally new to human thinking!

Christianity spread like wildfire because it declared forgiveness, truth, freedom from guilt, and release from the dark, depressing, harsh, and bleak expectations of life. It cleansed the conscience of failure, guilt, and shame and enabled the spirit of a person to realise their true worth and purpose in the sight of a gracious God. It birthed a new sense of expectation and excitement and inexplicable joy within the heart of man, as well as granting awareness of the reality of God's favour. Believers would live with God forever! Its appeal to the European population living within the dictates and whims of their rulers (very often to a person's social cost) was immense; there was more to life than what they could see around them! In short, Christianity gave not just hope but an expectant hope and a thrilling future through the realities of God's promises[lv] and the living confirmation of the Holy Spirit acting within an individual's own spirit. All this is beyond the scope of mere religion.

Initially, although Christianity was perceived as 'the enemy' in Rome, it proved to be both irresistible and unstoppable. Paul's letter to the Philippians includes a greeting from the 'household of Caesar' demonstrating that no one is immune to God's provision of goodwill—even household members of the Roman government had found answers to life in Christ! However, for the first three hundred years, apart from a few notably harsh exceptions, Christianity was merely endured by the Roman rulers. Rome's growth and success in the world had rested upon Roman military and organisational strength and their ability to subdue people and nations and maintain Roman authority. Although Christianity was literally unstoppable, the ruling powers were totally opposed to accept this new invasive philosophy liberating the oppressed people and nations. The general attitude of Roman rulers was perhaps exemplified in the statement by the emperor Trajan when replying to a query regarding Christians from Pliny, the governor of Bithynia:

'they must not be searched for, but if denounced and found guilty they must be punished.'[lvi]

There were six particularly brutal Roman emperors: Nero, around 64 CE, who, on trumped up charges, delighted in blaming Christians, wrapping them in animal skins, and setting vicious dogs on them; Marcus Aurelius around 160 CE, who is credited with 'surpassing intensity of all previous persecutions,'[lvii] (although most of the animosity could probably be attributed to informers); Decius who insisted on sacrifice being made to the Roman gods, which resulted in the genocide of Christians; Valerian specifically targeted Christians by insisting on sacrifice to Roman gods 257CE; Diocletian and Galerius (who ruled jointly circa 300CE), felt threatened by rising Christianity. Although, to be fair, it was during the reign of these malevolent emperors[lviii] that much of the persecution was at the behest of local governments and mobs rather than the emperors themselves.

Deaths were largely for the entertainment of the baying aggressive masses and involved being torn apart by wild animals, burned alive, crucified, or mutilated. Some were tortured and then sent to labour in Egyptian mines, or popular Christian 'friends' were granted a quick death by beheading. Ironically, it seems most of these particularly egregious emperors were killed soon after they prescribed or encouraged their plans of murderous torture.[lix]

The fact that so many Christians chose death over recantation demonstrates the life and power of the reality of God's presence and promises in the face of faith-based destruction. But this murderous malevolence did not last. Christianity grew and thrived throughout the Roman Empire until finally, in 313 CE, the Edict of Milan gave freedom of worship to all peoples. In 380 CE the emperor Constantine declared Christianity the national religion, ending Roman persecution.

With the relenting of physical persecution, surviving as a Christian became less and less a challenge to life. Over time, simple dynamic faith began to be organized into a sort of institution. Leading by the Spirit of God was replaced by seeking the opinions of those who had been close to at least one of the disciples of Christ, or even someone who knew someone who might have had contact with early Christianity— whoever was more senior in the faith. Since the beginning of Christianity, and with the removal of persecution, heresies and contrary opinions continually plagued the church. In the constant search for authoritative leadership, ultimately the bishop of Rome gained a larger following, and his opinion prevailed. He became known as 'the Pope' (Latin *Papa*). The earliest recorded use of the title *Pope* in English dates to the mid-tenth century, when it was used in reference to the seventh-century Roman Pope Vitalian in an Old English translation of Bede's *Historia ecclesiastical gentis Anglorum*.[lx]

As most of the European population was illiterate, the written Word of God was accessible to only a handful of priests. Thus, the true purpose for which Jesus died was gradually whittled down into the interpretations of a privileged few. Overall, interpretation was generally strictly monitored by the reigning pope, who organised the church into a personal hierarchy. On the face of it, this action appears suspicious, but God used the harsh authoritative methods of the Roman Catholic church to influence and control much of the world, frequently spreading the true gospel.

The Inquisition in Spain became a reign of terror in the New World. Temples were razed and idols were destroyed as aboriginal cultures were viewed as manifestations of the devil.[lxi]

Religious opinions began to warp the living message, and a hierarchy of functions gradually emerged and became the demand and proof of true Christianity. To some extent, this began to parallel the rules of Jewish law-keeping. Mankind has a proclivity to generate rules and regulations according to human perception, thereby subverting God's amazing revelation. The great truths that began the church were largely eroded for most people and altered or subverted over several hundred years.

First the physical headship of Jesus Christ was lost.

Subsequently the personal ministry of the Holy Spirit was largely replaced by opinions of people assumed to have comprehensive knowledge of God.

Leadership of the church became subjective; often military/physical struggles ensued to establish Christian seniority (at one point there were two Popes and later three Popes simultaneously, each purporting to be Christ's representative on earth).[lxii]

Vital truths of God's Kingdom were largely replaced with man's interpreted opinions.

Total immersion baptism gave way to sprinkling with a cup.

Infant baptism guaranteeing Christian identity began.

Finally, in 1095 CE Pope Urban II replaced salvation by God's grace with granting forgiveness to all who fought in the first crusade. Later the practice of 'purchasing indulgences' for relatives was allowed.[lxiii]

Regarding this last point, 'salvation' for one's dead loved ones became dependent upon paying money to the church to release them from purgatory, a religiously constructed, divine waiting room. This concept was in direct conflict to scripture that declared 'absence from the body is to be with Christ.'[lxiv] Peasants couldn't read the scriptures for themselves, so they would have no way of knowing scriptural accuracy anyway.

In 1184 CE, to remove all dissidents who expounded any understanding other than the Pope's edicts, Pope Lucius III issued the papal bull (ruling) *Ad abolendam*, which established tribunals authorising torture and death, mainly to combat the Albigensian heresy, which was deemed a threat to Roman Catholicism in southern France.

This murderous inquisition caught the imagination of several rulers and subsequent popes and was used for several hundred years, especially against other perceived heresies, such as the Cathars and the Waldensians. This enabled the Pope to maintain strict Roman Catholic control over the beliefs of the masses in Europe.

An ecclesiastical tribunal [was] established by Pope Gregory IX *c.* 1232 for the suppression of heresy. It was active chiefly in northern Italy and southern France, becoming notorious for the use of torture. In 1542 the papal Inquisition was revived to combat

Protestantism, eventually becoming an organ of papal government.[lxv]

Thus, for many hundreds of years, the true message of God's grace and love was obscured and the masses' access to salvation was controlled by man's contrived rules of true religion. All of which are meaningless when it comes to right living. Yet through all the obfuscation by man's will, God's love and deliverance flowed around the imprisoning bars of human contrivance to bring to many a sweet spiritual release and recognition and comfort of God's grace and peace. Amazing! Walking in the reality of God's presence transcends all human or satanic efforts at denial.

Even after the demise of Roman rule, the barbarian conquerors recognised the missionary monks throughout Europe to be bearers of a new faith and preservers of a higher civilization. There were great swings of power and domination throughout Europe, yet the gospel flowed to many people outside of these empire boundaries.[lxvi]

4

Christianity after the Middle Ages

It's impossible to clearly define the factors that contributed to the historical era known as the Renaissance. Perhaps it was a great weariness of the downtrodden peoples, or accumulation of events that inspired the hopes and aspirations of thinking people – or many other unseen reasons combined! But the start of the Renaissance was the beginning of fundamental and foundational changes throughout Europe.

The Renaissance was a fervent period of European cultural, artistic, political and economic "rebirth" following the Middle Ages. Generally described as taking place from the 14th century to the 17th century, the Renaissance promoted the rediscovery of classical philosophy, literature and art. Some of the greatest thinkers, authors, statesmen, scientists and artists in human history thrived during this era, while global exploration opened new lands and cultures to European commerce. The Renaissance is credited with bridging the gap between the Middle Ages and modern-day civilization.[lxvii]

The strangling grip of man's engineered religion was noticeably countered with the advent of both the Renaissance and the Reformation (religious reform), which occurred roughly during the same period. The Renaissance (French meaning 'rebirth') is, depending on the country, usually dated from the fourteenth to the seventeenth centuries. Both great movements occurred very slowly, initially in Italy and France, oozing gradually into the more northern countries. The Reformation was largely a release from religious dominance and the Renaissance allowed the exploration of history and development of art, music, mathematics, science, philosophy, and many other aspects of life. It allowed and encouraged free thinking and expression. It was an ethereal current of desire to escape the firmly maintained restrictions of life; an opportunity to use and develop God-given abilities, and a time of calculation and thought.

The Protestant Reformation was the 16th century religious, political, intellectual and cultural upheaval that splintered Catholic Europe, setting in place the structures and beliefs that would define the continent in the modern era. [lxviii]

Beginning roughly in the sixteenth century, the Reformation ultimately led to the formation of the Protestant religion, which broke away from Roman Catholicism. While occurring over decades, the Reformation was the irresistible force that gradually shifted the immovable object of the weight of Roman Catholicism from much of Europe. The minutia of the movement is unknown, but in 1517 CE, after Martin Luther proclaimed his ninety-five dissenting theses in Wittenberg refuting Roman Catholic errors and exposing the basis of papal lies, the common man became inspired to learn to read the Word of God. Concurrently, Huldrych Zwingli, in Austria, followed similar persuasion and promoted like opinions. Much later Jehan Cauvin (John Calvin) promoted concurring beliefs in France.

After studying the Chinese inventor Wang Zhen, Johannes Gutenberg designed and constructed the first European printing press in the fifteenth century, and printed his first book, the Bible on vellum, also known as calfskin. The British Library has estimated it would have taken about 170 calves to print one Bible, making it a very expensive book! Only about 180 Bibles were initially printed, and only a handful of those on vellum. The rest were on paper.

Following this however, Humanism, Schooling, and personal development began to flourish.[lxix] As education became commonplace, people were able to read for themselves that God's salvation came not through the edicts of the all-powerful Roman Catholic church, but through God's grace via faith (Sola fide [lat.]). The Holy Bible was first translated into English by William Tyndale, and the King James Bible was printed in 1611. This resulted in a far wider understanding of the precepts of the Word, which became more accessible. And so, the truth of God's miraculous gift began to break through the binding chains of human imposition.

The Protestant Church movement began as people gradually began to realise that God's word was not passed on by a mere man, but God's 'voice' could be heard by reading scripture for themselves. Although freedom and relief had come to the people of Europe through Christianity, mankind, being mankind, is all about control and manipulation, and many hundreds of years were characterised by the struggle between religious and political dominance.

For example, Charlemagne, king of the Franks, forcibly attempted to convert Saxons from their Germanic paganism by way of warfare. At the massacre of Verden, 782 CE, 4500 Germans who rebelled at the prospect of forced conversion to Christianity were killed. Similar actions have been attributed to King Charles II of Naples and Pope Innocent III.[lxx]

It is pertinent to note that Protestantism was never a single contained institution similar to the Roman Catholic church. It quickly fractured into many divisions, or denominations, as new truths were uncovered.

History of Protestantism[lxxi]

Over subsequent centuries, all the Christian truths that were originally lost to the church were restored, roughly in reverse order—beginning with Salvation by Grace alone. The only truth still outstanding is the restoration of the physical headship of Jesus Christ, which is soon to come!

As various differing truths from the Word of God were perceived by various people, differing threads of religion, or denominations, were formed. Usually, denominations are formed when a new truth is learned but the home church refuses to accept it. A split occurs, and the dissenting section of the congregation hives off, forming a new nest with a fresher understanding of certain parts of scripture. For example, John Wesley, in the eighteenth-century CE, felt appalled at the casual approach of the church towards Christianity. So, he gathered a group of followers around his understanding, and this group, which was generally mocked for its methods, eventually became known as 'Methodists'.[lxxii]

Around 1609 CE English speakers in Holland broke away for the Church of England adamant that infant sprinkling was wrong, and each individual believer should be baptised. This resulted in the formation of the Baptist denomination.[lxxiii] And this refining process resulting in denominational creation was repeated many times.

Now, the constant activity of the Spirit of God has been likened to a river flowing between the fixed, written banks of the Word of God.

At times the river is surging with powerful movement, and sometimes gentle. But it is always moving, and never stagnant. It is full of life and revelation but never overflowing the immovable banks of the Word of God.

Errors and problems arise when the unchecked spirit of man overlooks the instruction 'do not go beyond what is written'[lxxiv] and projects a perceived truth above all other truths, thus causing massive upheavals (floods) and competing priorities of understanding. Since the Reformation, this has resulted in intense antagonism between various denominations.

In order, the major denominations were:

Catholic and Orthodox	founded 1054	Western and Eastern Roman Empires
Reformed Presbyterian	founded 1520	Switzerland & Scotland
Lutheran	founded 1530	Germany
Anglican	founded 1534	Britain
Methodist	founded 1787	Britain [lxxv]

Other major families of denominations include Baptist, Methodist, Reformed churches (including Calvinism, Presbyterianism and Congregationalism), Lutheranism and Anabaptists (including Mennonites, Quakers, Church of the Brethren, Hutterites, Amish, and others).[lxxvi] There are various branches of mainline based churches that have developed into a Pentecostal style of understanding: Charismatic Catholics, Charismatic Lutherans, Charismatic Methodists or Charismatic whatever. They tend to promote a much friendlier approach to God and are therefore more expressive in their personal and congregational worship. Most of these denominations have sprung up in the twentieth century, long after the Reformation!

Most mainline churches are constrained by the 'riverbanks' of the Word of God, maintaining historically established doctrines, retaining liturgical services that prevent excess overflow of scriptural ideas. Pentecostal denominations on the other hand are largely based on the 'spirit of the river' as it flows along the solid banks of the Word God. Pentecostal churches focus more on the 'gifts of the Spirit'[lxxvii] and current transcendent revelation through the Word of God, differing from mainline churches. Although all belong to the family of God, they differ in their approach to God. Some maintain arm's length from each other through ritual and formal attitude, while others, such as some Pentecostals, see God as 'Daddy' and have no restraining barriers in their approach to God. Of late, these differences have mellowed, and a closer fellowship is experienced between Christians – whatever the denomination! Undoubtedly, regardless of differing religious understanding, the current 'social' leanings of societies have resulted in closer personal bonds of uncritical friendship.[lxxviii]

Christianity Expands

There are many maps and records of the burgeoning spread of Christianity throughout Europe, into Britain, North Africa, Asia, and even China, so it seems unnecessary to offer a geographical description here. Perhaps a notable example of European religious struggles was the birth of Belgium, in 1830, when the largely Catholic population of the south split away from the mainly Protestant population of Holland.[lxxix] However, this, of course, is long after our current focus.

The next notable move of Christianity came with European colonisation of much of the world. Starting around 1415 with Portuguese exploration in search of trade routes for Far East spices, native populations were subdued, and countries forcibly conquered by the superior use of gunpowder. However, along with aggressive colonisation, the Christian gospel was also spread amongst these original peoples. Africa, India, South Asia, and Brazil were subjected to the construction of various forts and factories which blossomed or were defeated at various times, but the underlying Christian influence remained. A physical force may be countered, but to restrain a transcendent idea is impossible.

Global Christian influence began, largely, with the Portuguese expansion of the Spanish Empire, especially notable in 1492 with the European 'discovery' of America and stretched through many areas of the world. Owing to its vast spread across the globe from east to west, the Spanish Empire was the first empire to be described as 'the empire upon which the sun never sets,' This descriptive title was later applied to the British Empire, which was by far the largest empire and affected about 23 percent of the world's population.[lxxx] There were other empires too, although not so large and influential, but an underlying result of these European empires was that Christianity spread throughout much of the world.

A considerable amount of the early Christian expansion into the world was carried out under the Roman Catholic religion, before the Protestant religion seriously existed. This is arguably because of their austere teaching methods, which were more severe than those of other Christian denominations. When the Roman Empire imploded, the Roman Catholic pope seized control of the Western Empire to avoid the collapse of Western civilization and Christianity.[lxxxi] Harsh methods such as the Inquisition were adopted over the years, to ensure faithfulness to the touted doctrines. This belligerent demeanour-maintained dominance ensured the Catholic religion would be the driving religious force behind territorial conquests. In the sixteenth century, Ignatius of Loyola founded the Jesuit Order and is recorded as saying, 'Give me a child till he's seven and I'll show you the man.'[lxxxii] This method of strict education was and still is imperative to continuance of religious purpose in many ways.

This mixing of religion and politics was also devastating to the Jews spread throughout the world. They were marginalised, massacred, bullied, and despised wherever they were found—and often labelled as 'Christ killers' within 150 years of the Crucifixion.

> **'God has been murdered; the King of Israel has been put to death by an Israelite right hand,'** wrote Melito, and popes, patriarchs, and pastors have echoed his words throughout the ages.[lxxxiii]

Even prominent theologians fell into this concept of Jewish guilt. Around 1271 CE, Thomas Aquinas wrote,

> **'It is true, as the laws declare that in consequence of their sin [of rejecting and crucifying Jesus] the Jews were destined to perpetual servitude, so that sovereigns of states may treat Jewish goods as their own property'.** [lxxxiv]

And so right down to modern days:

> **'As for the Jews, I am just carrying on with the same policy which the Catholic Church had adopted for 1500 years,'** Chancellor Hitler wrote to Bishop Berning in April 1933.[lxxxv]

But through all these invasive expansions Christianity spread throughout most of the world, bringing the amazing satisfaction of release from sin's condemnation. Faithful, dedicated missionaries also followed up to bolster the Christian message, but unfortunately this relief was often also mixed with the harsh dictates of colonial masters, producing a sort of mixed blessing. In a strange way, that helped the spread of the gospel, because just as high pressure creates diamonds, so concentrated tribulation constructs solid and valuable Christian beliefs. A notable example of this was the growth of Christianity amongst the future black slaves of the American cotton fields. Undoubtedly this is because of the tribulation that forces a person to seek transcendent relief. In the words of C. S. Lewis,

> **'God whispers to us in our pleasures, speaks in our conscience, but shouts in our pain: it is His megaphone to rouse a deaf world.'**[lxxxvi]

However, too much enduring political and religious pressure in Europe caused dissatisfaction and discomfort, and so the 'newly discovered' Americas appeared to provide a fertile place for a new start. Resultingly, settlements sprang up in the Americas at various times. The Spanish conquistadors moved into South America in the early sixteenth century to make or find their fortunes, and they brought the Roman Catholic religion with them. Also, in the sixteenth century the French moved into Canada and North America, again bringing mainly the Roman Catholic religion.

5

Christianity in America

The American continent was a place of possibility for Europeans.[lxxxvii] Although the Viking, Lief Erikson briefly touched on the American continent in 1000 CE, it was not until the European 'discovery' of America by the Italian Christopher Columbus, in 1492, that escaping the political malevolence and warfare of Europe became a real possibility. This, however, was not a simple matter of transference!

In 1507 CE this new world came to be known as America, named after Italian merchant Amerigo Vespucci (Latin, *Americus Vespucius*) who explored for Spain and Portugal. France and Spain made several attempts to settle North America but were unable to maintain their presence due to native resistance, lack of supplies, and sicknesses. In fact, there were more than ten attempts to establish settlements in North America, all of which initially failed for various reasons. However, Spanish conquistadors moved successfully into South America and, in time, filtered up the west coast of North America.[lxxxviii] Portugal also made great inroads into South America,

Notable too was the French entry into Canada in 1534, by Jacques Cartier, who mapped the St. Laurence River and Gulf. (The Vikings are reputed to have landed in America long before this, and, on the west coast, the Haida Indians around the Vancouver area portrayed a similar Viking lifestyle of aggression up and down the coast.) But the French entrance seemed purely to obtain furs for export to Europe. They also penetrated the North American hinterland.

The first successful settlement in North America came with the English arrival of 104 men and boys at Jamestown in 1607. Within a few years it was on the brink of extinction, but by 1612 it developed into a workable community. The inclusion of women in 1619 made[lxxxix] it into a thriving community. **Women were known to provide a sense of stability.**[xc]

It seemed to cancel the purpose of merely 'raping' the countryside for the benefit of the motherland, and with the inclusion of women began a feeling in the Jonestown settlers wanting to establish their own communities. In their initial struggles to survive, the settlers met in a church and established the House of Burgesses that same year, which controlled legislative procedure and could be addressed to settle grievances and legal disputes. For the first time in history outside of Judaism, every individual had some sort of recognised rights and personal value.

The Dutch East India Company was chartered by the Dutch Republic to establish a foothold in America. Their first established settlement was in 1615, and they went on to establish New Amsterdam in 1626, which was later sold to the British to become New York. [xci]

Britain later founded thirteen colonies on the east coast of Northern America, fundamentally established to return wealth back to Britain. Ironically, most of the settlers came to America largely to escape from the political corruption of governments and the Anglican Church. Much of all the settlement from other countries had this reasoning in their purpose.[xcii]

Following the war of American Independence (1775-1783 CE) and motivated by the concern that the young country might collapse, the American constitution came into force in 1789 CE and begins with the words, 'We the People,' signifying that the old European customs of kingship, feudalism, and unfair dominance were no longer recognised or countenanced. No one could be condemned for their beliefs or speech, and freedom of worship without persecution was legislated. The British Magna Carta was instrumental in the construction of the American constitution. Although exceedingly difficult in many instances, daily living became different to anywhere else in the world. By liberating people to openly follow their heart's directives while subjected to moral and legal community laws, the American people made advances that liberated their thinking and practices more than any nation on earth. They also included inscribing the phrase 'In God We Trust' on their currency.

Although basic Christian morals prevailed, religion was to be kept separate from politics. America became arguably the greatest Christian country in the world, and according to God's instruction to the Jews in Deuteronomy 28:1 (ESV), 'If you faithfully obey the voice of the Lord your God, being careful to do all his commandments that I command you today, the Lord your God will set you high above all the nations of the earth.' America certainly outstripped the rest of the world in most areas. Even though there has always been some form of corruption in the country, God has nevertheless been true to his word as America has fostered principles engendered by Christ. Even with the current level of corruption in the government and people, today there are arguably more solid Christians than in any other western nation. America has been recorded as sending out the most Christian missionaries to spread the great news of Christ's redeeming offer to sin-bound individuals.[xciii]

In reality, all men have God's moral law contained within each person's being, because God said He would write His Law on every heart.[xciv] His voice can be heard through one's conscience; effective depending upon whether it is obeyed or allowed to be diverted by selfish desires and other means of attraction. Regrettably, modern attractions, human logic, and media have numbed much of influence of the conscience. But the young America made it a principle not to allow European history and influence to dictate their worldview. And God demonstrated his pleasure by making America successful.

Another significant fact that highlights America as the only truly Christian country from its foundation was the construction of the Washington Monument, the world's tallest obelisk, built in two stages around 1750 and 1790. Amongst the items buried at its base is a Holy Bible and a copy of the 1789 Constitution, and on the east face of the aluminium cap at the top of the monument is inscribed the Latin words *Laus Deo,* meaning 'Praise be to God.' It is positioned to catch the first rays of the morning sun before the rest of the capital city. This, in précis, reveals the original heart and Christian intent of the nation.[xcv]

Throughout American history, there has always been a thread of Christian principles and morals, but it seems at this moment that Christianity is under great assault in America. The voices of socialism and chaos have become loud of late, and there are incidences of cheating and gross corruption in American politics, subverting their original objectives. It cannot be accurately predicted as to the influence this will have in defining the downgrading of American influence in the world, but it is pertinent to remember that God's calendar revolves around Israel, and the principle of 'whoever blesses you I will bless' remains. So long as America supports Israel, America will survive! So long as there is no Rapture (or removal) of the church, America will survive. But with so many Christians in America removed at the Rapture, the country will collapse. The church will survive without America, but America will not survive without the church![xcvi]

Speaking of moral issues, in one sense Western civilization reached its peak around the 1950s and 1960s CE! From this point, a permeating seepage of corruption began to dominate world nations and societies as American might, money, and lifestyle captured their collective national foci, slowly but noticeably. Following the Second World War, a subtle shift of priorities became evident within the world's populations. Teaching godly morals became less and less important. As one generation was given little of immense value regarding morals, they had little to pass on to their children, and so on from generation to generation until now, when expediency has practically replaced many godly morals. Strong, definitive American Christian influence has begun steadily to decline throughout the world.

Technology, manufacturing, clothing, and social esteem began to occupy and demand greater attention as they seemed to suggest the possibility of unheard-of progress. Slowly but steadily values began to change. Entertainment has seized the attention of the youth, and they are more noticeably revered by adults who regard them with inflated value. Teaching children godly morals began increasingly to slip by the wayside. Abortion and immorality have skyrocketed, and from 1984, with the evolution of the internet, access to endless opinions on any subject proliferates the public square. Youth have become a major influence in communities.

In a sense, with the advent of the public internet, there has come a re-birth of the Tower of Babel, which proposes enslavement of all men with a common ideal of replacing God with social values. Even traditionally established history is being snidely rewritten, in some areas. In this regard the true motive is opaque, to say the least. It could, perhaps, be implied that the internet is the extension of man's downfall, mirroring the Tower of Babel. When they crucified Jesus, he said to those weeping at the injustice of his situation, Luke 23:27-31 PARA "Don't weep for me. Weep for yourselves. If this is what happens when the tree is green, imagine what it will be like when the tree is dry (the growth of injustice and sin with the passing of time and the expansion of evil). The time is coming when you will prefer death to life."

However, all this is no surprise. Jesus prophesied of these disturbances that in the last days, famines, pestilences, and earthquakes around the world would increase and many would falter in their Christian belief. He also revealed that Christianity would come under great pressure, and the murder of Christians would abound. Jesus spoke of many turning their back on following him, but also spoke of the whole world being exposed to the gospel before he returns to collect his followers – people still clinging earnestly to his salvation as they become aware of his love and plan, and finally recognising there are no dependable truths or promises in the current world climate.

He said, 'When you see these things happening, pack your bags. Redemption is coming.'[xcvii]

> **And as soon as the grain is ready, the farmer comes and harvests it with a sickle, for the harvest has come!**'[xcviii]

6

Grand Finale

The finalisation of Christianity is a rock-solid, documented promise of Jesus Christ[xcix] – and he cannot lie! Christianity will end with the Rapture – or removal of the Church (from this world's presence and control), and newly-awakened Jews will resume their original mandate of reaching out to the world's nations.[c]

There has been discussion regarding whether or not there will really be a Rapture or merely that everyone will meet Jesus Christ at his return. Well, Jesus cannot lie, and he stated that he would build his church and 'all the powers of hell will not conquer it.' (NLT) However, the Book of Revelation records that the antichrist is, 'allowed to wage war against God's holy people and to conquer them'. As Christ cannot lie, the Church cannot be on earth at this point, only the proselytes of the Jewish evangelists.[ci]

Although this expected event is prophetical and impossible to calculate in occurrence or time, we can, nevertheless, estimate much of its fulfilment by observing world conditions. Perhaps the most obvious indicators centre on the Jewish nation, and are found in the Apostle Paul's letter to the Romans,

'Has God cast away his people? Certainly not!'[cii]

Paul goes on to show how God temporarily sidelined the Jews for a season (a God-allowed timeframe),

'Until the full number of Gentiles comes to Christ. And so all Israel will be saved,'[xiii] (See chapter 2 'A Change of Track' which details how and when the Jews were temporarily sidelined in favour of the Gentiles.)

This confirms what Jesus said to the Jews in Matthew chapter twenty-three, [civ]

'Your house is abandoned and desolate … you will never see me again until you say, "Blessings on the one who comes in the name of the Lord!"'

In other words, after the removal of the gentile Church the Jewish nation will recognise Jesus as their expected Messiah, and the Jews once again become prominent. Quite obviously, with the disappearance of Christianity from the earth, people left behind will become extremely attentive to the preaching of the 144,000 Jewish evangelists who have newly awakened to the risen Christ.[cv] However, it would appear from the description of Rev. chapter seven that all their converts will die for their faith, as the world leader, termed antichrist, will have God's permission to overcome them. Having realised the truth of God's plan, and seeking the blood -covering of Jesus' sacrifice, they will prefer death to what they know will be coming.

Thereafter, Revelation chapter nine describes world-wide warfare on a scale never-before seen, resulting in the death and murder of a third of the world's population. Under current logistics, this would account for the deaths of around two to three billion people.

It's possible that after realising the truth of the situation and having seen the removal of the Christian Church that these murdered masses could be the martyr converts of the Jewish evangelists, referred to in

Revelation chapter 7:9-14. This, of course is merely conjecture, but very possible. While this seems unlikely to occur under conventional warfare methods it could conceivably happen through nuclear warfare, or by another means of mass destruction. The world is presently bristling with various countries possessing nuclear armaments, all threatening their immediate use. Another possibility may be verified by the Apostle Peter, who writes that on God's Day he will,

> **'Set the heavens on fire. And the elements will melt away in flames.**[cvi]

Of course, this explanation is also conjecture, but it is very possible too! We know that the rapture will happen, because God cannot lie, but we are not clear as to the timing or the method.

The Bible also mentions God sending a lie upon the earth to deceive those who determinedly resist his offer.[cvii]

7

In Closing

To set the background; the world will be manoeuvred into the grasp of a handful of governments, which will be manipulated by one man, whom the Bible refers to as the antichrist.[cviii] He will have total control over all humans, their life practices, buying and selling abilities, political and religious beliefs, and will demand total worship. He will declare himself as God, and murder anyone who dissents.

The main purpose and focus of the antichrist will be to destroy the Jews. Probably because Israel will have a vast and influential input into world affairs, which will challenge and annoy the antichrist. After the fulfilment of God's promise to restore the Jews back into Israel, God has allotted a seven-year period for final Jewish influence called the Tribulation, or the time of Jacob's trouble.[cix] During the first three-and-a-half years many Jews will travel throughout the world speaking of God's grace and mercy. They will have a remarkably successful witness, but all will be killed for their faith. Referred to above, these innumerable tribulation martyrs are specifically mentioned in Revelation chapter seven.

Initially, the antichrist will make a pact, or treaty with Israel for seven years, allowing the Jews to be very active in reaching out to the world, but halfway through he will resent Jewish influence, and his forces will storm into Israel to begin a mass genocide of Jews, destroying two thirds of them. It is likely the surviving third will escape to the Jordan area of the Middle East, beyond the reach of the antichrist.[cx]

I deal with this time of closing history in my book 'Entity'. The final three and a half years is dealt with in Revelation chapters nine to eighteen, and nineteen closes history. (currently withdrawn for editing.)

It is during these final years that God will pour out his wrath upon the earth affecting everything from stars to water. It will be a very unpleasant time.

This whole political scene will be overthrown by the return of Jesus Christ who will crush the antichrist and his followers, bringing about a totally new world order, the like of which has never before been witnessed.

Part 2

God Loves you but...

Two Kingdoms Currently Exist

(Revealed through the Gospel in five colours)

1 **Gold** – Kingdom of Theology
2 **Black** – Kingdom of Depravity

3 **Red** – Salvation – the way of escape
4 **White** – Justification
5 **Green** – Sanctification
6 **The Plan**

   Part A – Adam to Day of the Lord

   Part B – Training – Regardless, you are going to experience hurt

   Part C – the final touch, or the second centimetre of our tape measure

The Two Kingdoms

In Part 1 we looked at Christian history and the anticipated finalisation of Christian and current human-controlled history. In this part we will examine the meaning and purpose of life through the lens of the Gospel. We will also look, so much as we are able, at God's eternal plan for creation.

Perhaps the most gripping fact of life is that everyone of us is an eternal being, designed to exist forever!^{cxi}

Did you get that? You and I are going to exist forever!

Oh, our bodies will die, but the real you – thoughts, personality, demeanour, everything that consists of you and me will live forever. As eternal beings our life on earth is merely the brief training ground for entrance to eternity. Our responsibility is a matter of choosing in which kingdom to reside for eternity, and the quality of that life. Generally speaking, eternal life's quality depends on our willing obedience to God's prescribed plan, and actions to doing what is right: our actions here on earth are more important than we think. This short lifespan on earth requires that we each train our minds to do the best we can achieve, according to God's expectation of us.

The battlefield of life lies largely in the mind, where sin takes root. This results because physical actions usually spring from the focus of our thoughts.^{cxii} What we allow to occupy our minds eventually becomes our personal demeanour. The conclusion of our future therefore lies in the matter of choosing in which kingdom to reside for eternity and to change our thinking and attitude to qualify.

Now, regarding action for citizenship, to more accurately illustrate this point, let's say moving to America equivalates to the optimal and most comfortable life choice. Alternatively, a socialist country is the other choice, where, even with our willingness to conform, there is lack of protection, and life is tenuous and tentative, and law and order is subjective. Whichever choice we prefer, we will have to follow a procedure. First, we will need to apply for approval of acceptance from that desired country, and having achieved that, we will have to pack up our life and lifestyle and physically move to the country of our choice. Simply telling everybody our preference won't make us a citizen.

Let's substitute that scenario with reality. There are two existing eternal kingdoms which affect our future: the Kingdom of Gold, or Theology, (where we want to be) and the Kingdom of Black, or Depravity. (Which is where we are)

The first is the perfect choice because of its ruler - He once revealed information about his character and demeanour and clearly revealed that his Kingdom functions through morals – doing what is right and beneficial to all! The Kingdom of Theology (Theo = about God; ology = learning about) is completely superb and therefore coloured gold. Jesus doesn't merely give life, peace, and joy. Jesus embodies life peace and joy. That's who he is. Therefore, the deeper one's relationship with Jesus, the more life, peace and joy will emanate from that person. Everyone who is part of this Kingdom is always joyful and prospers – even after the initial shock of hard circumstances! Relationship with Jesus Christ is imperative. Jesus underscored, '**I am the way…**'[cxiii]

Gold – Kingdom of Theology

The first recorded instance of God revealing the specifics of himself, and his Kingdom were to Moses, who lived around 1300 BCE. This can be read in the book of Exodus.

> **"The Lord passed in front of Moses, calling out,**
> **Yahweh! The Lord!**
> **The God of Compassion and mercy!**
> **I am slow to anger and filled with unfailing love and**
> **faithfulness.**
> **I lavish unfailing love to a thousand generations. I**
> **forgive iniquity, rebellion, and sin.**
> **But I do not excuse the guilty** (unconfessed sin).

I lay the sins of the parents upon their children and grandchildren; the entire family is affected – even children in the third and fourth generations." [cxiv]

So much for his demeanour, and therefore the nature of his Kingdom. God doesn't merely 'love' – He is love. And he loves unconditionally. But unconditional love does not inspire maturity in its recipients. Maturity develops with challenges to life and compliance to instruction. Handling these challenges promotes justice, fairness, and doing what is morally good for self and for others. God stipulated the following moral requirements to exist in his kingdom:

1. Make sure God is your most intimate companion and lawgiver: -
2. Take care not to allow anyone or anything to supersede this relationship between you and God: -
3. Never do anything wrong or shady and try to pass it off as 'condoned by God'. There will be consequences![cxv] : -
4. Keep God's instructions as your everyday focus and concentrate on helping others: -
5. Take special pains to honour your parents: -
6. Don't murder: -
7. Don't touch another person's spouse: -
8. Don't pilfer or steal: -
9. Never denigrate or lie about another person: -
10. Don't yearn after something or someone belonging to another person.[cxvi]

What else do we know about this perfect kingdom?

When God instructed Moses to build the Ark of the Covenant and the Tabernacle, He insisted that almost everything contained gold of some sort. Gold represents complete, precious value.

God instructed that the priest's clothes contain various articles of gold. In fact, everything Moses was instructed to do contained gold and even when they constructed the golden calf, the wayward people of Israel recognised that Deity must be represented by gold. When the Philistines rulers realised that they had offended God they sent a gold offering from their god in hopes of appeasing the God of Israel.

And when it comes to generosity, God demonstrates he is inexplicably kind, to lavish his generosity upon everyone:

**He causes his sun to rise on the evil and the good, and
sends rain on the righteous and the unrighteous** [cxvii]

And as he conceded to David the king that had it been necessary, He would have given David much more than he had. David himself acknowledges that God had placed a crown of finest gold on David's head. In fact, God promised his people,

**I will exchange your bronze for gold
your iron for silver
your wood for bronze,
and your stones for iron.
I will make peace your leader
and righteousness your ruler violence will
disappear from your land;
the desolation and destruction of war will end.
Salvation will surround you...** [cxviii]

Not only that, but God promises to never fail or abandon us, and to be present with us through all of life's difficulties.

There's only one problem: no-one can qualify to enter the Kingdom of Gold because we are all sinners. **'Everyone has sinned, and we all fall short of God's glorious standard.'**[xxix] Tragically, we have only to break one of God's entrance requirements, once, to disqualify our eligibility! And, quite apart from that, we are all born infected with sin. Sin is inherent.

What an enigma! God states he has provided that every person ever born should enter his Kingdom of Theology, but this can only occur only after spiritual rebirth! Corrupt human flesh will never enter the Kingdom of Gold!

Imagine you hold in your hand a glass of water and you drop one tiny speck of fetid, human excrement into the glass. Would you drink it?

Neither will God allow one speck of sin into his kingdom. And we are all infected with sin! God's intention for each of us is totally unknown to us. It does not even enter the thoughts of natural man the plan God has for each individual.[cxx] Natural mankind is totally focused on this visible life. One of the only unexplained things is that all people have a niggling feeling that there is more to their future than what is visible or conceivable.[cxxi]

Jesus said:

I assure you no-one can enter the kingdom of God without being born (again) **of water and the spirit.**[cxxii]

In other words, not even a shadow of suspicion, or a hint of questionable honesty can enter this kingdom. It was tried once by a pride-filled, power-crazed angel by the name of Lucifer. He was created by God as a splendid being, an amazing specimen, making him supreme amongst the angel host. His heavenly history can be read in the book of Ezekiel chapter twenty-eight. Lucifer was absolutely glorious in all of

God's creation. Ezekiel records him as being the 'seal of perfection', with complete access to God's kingdom and supreme authority overall. But Lucifer rose up in pride and self-adulation, desiring to supersede God. In Isaiah we read Lucifer's rebellion resulted in him being banished from Heaven's Kingdom to earth, where he established his own kingdom in implacable opposition to God's eternal values.

But this promotes a question; why did a compassionate and merciful God confine Lucifer to earth together with his children, and not merely remove him?

Simply put, it was to ensure we could learn to resist Lucifer's sinful influence, and through instruction, personal trial, test, and perseverance, grow up to mirror God's son, Jesus.[cxxiii] More on this below.

Imagine, if you will, allowing just one termite into a wooden frame house. It will quickly attract other termites, and in time you will realise the integrity of the building's structure has been seriously compromised! Imagine what that would be like over the length of eternity and the number of termites there would be. Similarly, just as failure to remove even one weed in your garden results in an outbreak of weeds. Likewise, imagine if sin were allowed into the kingdom of Theology.

No, not even one sin is allowed in the Kingdom of Theology. Lucifer's one aim is to corrupt all mankind through the influence and power of sin! That's why he was ousted from God's Kingdom. God's unconditional love continuously spurned and rejected is eventually overtaken by justice.

Black Kingdom of Depravity

The kingdom that Lucifer, also called Satan, set up on earth is best identified by the colour black and named Depravity. This is because it is constructed with insanity, deceit, jealousy, destruction, murder, sickness, intrigue, deception, vileness – all the ugly characteristics listed throughout the Bible and manifested daily in our lives. Jesus summed it up by describing, 'The thief's purpose is to steal, and kill, and destroy.' In simple terms, it appears certain that in a complete and utter display of jealousy and malicious malevolence, Lucifer was enraged that Adam was given control of the world, and he, the awesome one, was not. He therefore decided to destroy God's creation, man and the whole of God's world. As a result of his subtle deception resulting in Adam's foolish and selfish actions, death and destruction infected all earthly life. Jesus revealed Lucifer/Satan as a murderer and the father of lies from the beginning. Satan is so skilled at deception that much of the world doesn't even believe he exists![cxxiv] General thought would have us believe that this current life we live is normal. This is all there is! No cause for alarm. Nothing to see here!

To further explain, the earth is also home to humanity, and, to begin with, it seems strange that God would send Satan to the same place as his human masterpiece creation. There is a purpose for this, which will be discussed shortly. When the earth was created, Adam, the first man, was instructed to oversee and manage God's creation and to name all the animals, which he did.

He was also instructed never to eat fruit from a certain tree, or source. At some point Satan appeared, in disguise as a serpent, to Eve, Adam's wife, and by deception convinced Eve of the veracity of his statements regarding the value of this tantalizing fruit. Thus, she favoured her own judgement above God's instruction. When Adam decided to follow Eve's action, his stewardship of the earth was forfeited to Satan, who, by Christ's admission, became ruler of the earth.

This process is, perhaps, made easier to understand by the following metaphorical image:

Picture a perfect Artic Supreme peach hanging from a tree. It is huge and juicy, with beautiful rosy skin, looking absolutely delicious. See a nectar feeding insect alight on the perfect skin of the peach, injecting its eggs into the body of the peach. In time, the eggs hatch and the worms grow, feeding on the perfect peach body. The integrity of the peach visibly alters.

The colour changes. The character softens. Fruit flies are attracted to the weeping flesh and feed and lay more eggs. It drops from the tree onto the ground where it attracts worms, caterpillars, ants, and anything that fancies it. Finally, the mushy smelly mess on the ground is a blight to the character of the tree and must be removed and discarded.

The peach is no longer healthy or desirable, fit only for the garbage heap!

In exactly the same way, Satan's deception simultaneously infused Adam and all his subsequent descendants with an infection of sin, the essence of Satan. His body began to decay, and his sin-corrupted eternal spirit estranged him from association with the Kingdom of Theology. Satan's sin nature became his sin nature, affecting all his descendants. His impaired spiritual nature earmarked his destiny as a precursor to the eternal garbage heap.

Currently we live in a logical world where spiritual understanding is virtually non-existent, where every physical facet of life is humanly interpreted and naturally reasoned, in some form or another. However, there are facts in life that are a conundrum to natural explanation and are more commonly explained by guesswork and shrugged shoulders. Many characteristics of life show we are actually part of something much bigger and these are witnessed through our conscience; awareness of right and wrong, our ability to think, our ability to choose actions and reactions, our emotions that often vary for no logical reason, irresistible and innate recognition of fairness, and the bent within our spirit to individually achieve something. These testify that we are designed for a higher purpose. Fear of death also alerts us to something unnatural in our human existence.

We know the earth is magnetic because this is the principle that enables compasses to function. Magnets are able to attract and repel. How is it that gravity only attracts?

Jesus Christ acknowledged Satan's control of this world when he was tempted by Satan in the desert. At that time Satan offered him possession of the earth, on condition Jesus worshiped him above God. (BTW. Satan's motive to control God was thereby openly revealed!) Jesus didn't refute Satan's right to give the earth, thereby confirming Satan's current temporary ownership. To his own disciples He also confirmed Satanic dominance of the world, by saying the 'ruler of this world approaches (but) he has no power over me.'

However, the sobering fact remains that all humanity is situated on earth within the kingdom of Depravity. In the West, especially, we are a people consumed with distraction and entertainment, and we love and make allowance for our favourite sins. We bump from attraction to attraction without considering the purpose and brevity of our current life on earth, which is being carefully monitored by a loving God, who is minutely and compassionately watching over his children. At some point, this entire kingdom of Depravity will be removed from the earth, including everyone and everything in it, all linked together by chains of habit, deception, and misconception.

This current lifestyle, or Kingdom of Depravity, is listed in the Bible to be removed to the Lake of Fire. God's love, which in spite of sin, is presently enabling friendship, kindness, goodness, and gratitude on the earth, will no longer be available. Life apart from God will be filled with distrust, suspicion, fear, panic, and alarm. Jesus spoke of this final state of the Kingdom of Depravity as a furnace of "wailing and gnashing of teeth" – otherwise described as misery and deep regret, perhaps encapsulated in the horrific thought, 'if only I had thought it through'.

Eternity's existence would have been inestimably superior had delayed gratification been employed – wait for the best, don't settle for rubbish! Unfortunately, human nature's inclination towards immediate expediency has largely and effectively replaced God's prescribed eternity for humankind.

The cause of most of man's unhappiness is sacrificing
what he wants most for what he wants now.[cxxv]

As mentioned above, each member of mankind is an eternal soul, but can never enter God's kingdom, because not only were we born in sin, but each one of us sins every single day and will do till the day our body dies. Sin is not error learned from external forces. Sin is imbedded in the human psyche from birth and is defined and refined through time, outside influence and natural proclivity. The Bible indicates that after death comes judgment.

Regarding innate corruption, have you ever met even a mere toddler, surrounded by their mess, who will acknowledge authorship of the mess? What about crayon scribbles on the walls? When asked if they did this, they would invariably shake their head and say, 'No'! Or deflect blame for the current mishap. We are each born innately infested with sin.[cxxvi]

Lying and self-deception are natural instincts of human nature. Which is actually amazing! Originally, mankind was made in God's image and is still capable of inventing, constructing, and achieving incredible things. Consider this: dissatisfaction with the status quo has motivated mankind to diligently search for cures for illnesses. Moral dissatisfaction led to the abolishment of slavery, and also to accountable government. In the words of Dennis Prager,

'In the personal realm, human dissatisfaction is what
makes personal improvement possible.'[cxxvii]

So, we can see that humankind has the ability to comprehend and procure amazing advantages for life's improvement. And yet, all people are so infected with sin, each and every person is capable of indescribable evil. Inventions designed to help and assist the human race are soon turned to means of destruction – e.g. nuclear power. What a contradiction! And God hates it all. No-one is worthy, yet everyone is acceptable to God – but only through identification with Jesus: by procuring salvation eligibility, and obedience to his directions. In mechanical terms, there is only one train that will ever make it to heaven's station. That train is Jesus. If we want to see heaven's shore, stay on the train!

'No one comes to the Father except through me'. – Jesus Christ[cxxviii]

How sad it is that mankind fell from the original estate, yet how incredibly amazing that God should establish a means of regaining even more than the original estate!

Red Salvation – the way of escape

God looked down from his eternal perfection and saw fallen mankind struggling in sin, sickness and depravity, with no opportunity to escape from the final destiny of the kingdom of Depravity.

God therefore sent Jesus to deal with the issue.[cxxix]

Jesus laid aside his deity and was born uniquely by the Spirit of God into human's inherited fleshly corruption – but not of Adam's failed dynasty. He was a special creation using 'Adam's' flesh but not his failed spiritual corruption.[cxxx]

God declared him to be the eternal High Priest, but in order to be high priest for man, it necessitated he should also be a man.[cxxxi]

Jesus lived his life facing identical weaknesses, potential failures and temptations common to all people, but without fault. He was never deceived as Adam had allowed himself to be. He healed all who came to him, comforted the oppressed, and brought the light of God's Word to the psychologically and emotionally imprisoned. Jesus demonstrated how to live a blameless life in a fallen world. He told his disciples that he had come to fulfill and complete the Old Testament Covenant and to be the sacrifice on behalf of fallen man to free them from the penalty of Satan's corruption and lies. Jesus said that he had authority to lay down his own life, and that no-one could take it from him. He also had authority to take it up again.

After his exemplary life, Jesus allowed himself to be crucified and died to pay the required penalty for man's sin and failure. This act of crucifixion ended Adam's fallen line by nailing every past sin and potential accusation against humankind to the cross.[cxxxii] He died as the last of failed 'Adam's progeny', because all people now have the opportunity to be with him in His resurrection, as a new creation. And in accordance with biblical prophecy, Jesus rose on the third day. It was by the shedding of his totally innocent blood that salvation was procured for humankind! Hence his shed blood became the new covenant for all men, replacing the Jewish only covenant of the Old Testament. He is the sole means of escape of the final future of life as we know it. It is through accepting and believing God's promises we become partakers of the divine nature.[cxxxiii]

Following his resurrection from the dead, Jesus again saw over five hundred of his disciples for forty days. He told them that He was returning to heaven to intercede with God on their behalf, and he would send the Holy Spirit in his place. So, get to know him; make a friend of him; he will show you how to live and what to do.

He then rose into the clouds with a promise he would return to collect his followers.

If the Black Kingdom of Depravity, commencing with this reasonable current lifestyle, seems preferable to you, there is no entry requirement. Just live on in your common current understanding and practice of life. We are all citizens already. However, at the end of the age the kingdom of Depravity and all who follow its demands and values will be swept into the Lake of Fire. From there, with the availability of God's loving demeanour removed, things will go rapidly downhill.

However, if you prefer to reject the Kingdom of Darkness and Depravity,[cxxxiv] then understand, believe and acknowledge Jesus rose from the dead and lives.[cxxxv] He will transfer you into His marvellous understanding, where you will be able to commune with Him in a way that is beyond your comprehension. Ask him to rule your life and tell others of your decision. Openly confess your changed belief and keep reading the Word of God. Through it, God will talk to you through your conscience. Whenever you sin and follow your own selfish desires (and you will), confess your mistake to God, who mercifully promised to forgive you (whatever you've done) and enable you to follow him once more.

White Justification

It's an indescribable experience to realise the value of God's salvation. As awareness of this transaction becomes fact, the reality of God's presence becomes tangible and the feeling of being forgiven becomes a massive load removed from our back. In our heart we realise the truth that Jesus Christ has risen from the dead and now resides in our deepest understanding, as a friend – not an enemy!

In time, if not immediately, we begin to realise how little we really know about the things of God. Talking with other Christians becomes imperative, and the desire to know more about Jesus and his intentions, keeps growing.

Talking to others, and sharing our changing worldview, becomes a must do! Depending on the character and nature of each believer, this type of thinking may happen immediately or occur gradually. However, God intends it to definitely happen at some point in a believer's life.

The result of God moving in the believer's life is recorded in 1 Peter 2:9. He has taken us out of the kingdom of Depravity and into His marvellous light. And what a light this is! Our life's previous attitudes, focus, and expectations lose their hold; the issues that always seemed so imperative now fade into the background of our intentions – a new focus is apparent. God puts a song in our heart, and we feel we just have to let it out. Joy fills our heart more and more. We have 'put on Christ'[cxxxvi] - we have become a page in His Story, His book. Jesus is real! The old has gone: the new has come![cxxxvii] We have received the guaranteed entry approval to the Kingdom of Gold.

Because the new believer is not instantly, physically swept into God's Kingdom of Gold, there is a commonly expressed idea that God has withdrawn from mankind to watch what happens, from a distance: this is totally fallacious! In the words of Jesus, recorded in Joh 5:17 (NIV) **'My Father is always at his work to this very day, and I too am working,'** Just as a silversmith carefully and attentively watches over their melting inspiration, to skim off the impurities, so God watches his charges. From a completely sinful and depraved human mass, God daily applies small pressures to engender decisions from every individual person to do what is right, or to choose to do wrong; to either turn to God or turn away from God. Occasionally, there are spectacular demonstrations of unimaginable miraculous healings or events. But more commonly, life consists of nuances in thought or speech that demand our human response.

We are faced, every day, with choices requiring reaction. There are opportunities to promote or withhold our own perceptions. There are challenges to condone or condemn speeches and actions. There are people to assess and either check or encourage. Every day is replete with choices. Whichever we decide may be right or wrong because Colossians 3:15 urges us to allow the peace of Christ to arbitrate or umpire our decision. In other words, 'do the right thing' in God's estimation.

Our conscience will tell us whether or not we have made the right decision. We are daily faced with decisions to do right or to err. Knowing

God's Word, prayer, and church fellowship will clarify these decisions. Obedience will sharpen our understanding and strengthen our character. Blatant disregard of our conscience will destroy our faith.

Jesus faced exactly the same choice. Matthew 26:53, 54 (NIV) record what Jesus could have done to defend himself, **(Do you think I cannot call on my Father, and he will at once put at my disposal more than twelve legions of angels?)** but also reveals his determination to do what he knew to be right **(But how then would the Scriptures be fulfilled that say it must happen in this way?)** Verses 38-42 reveal his struggle and decision to block out his personal preference in favour of doing what was right. **("My Father, if it is not possible for this cup to be taken away unless I drink it, may your will be done.")**

By way of a small personal example of the work of the Holy Spirit, when I was looking to buy a house, I was shown two side-by-side properties with mirror-designed houses being built on each property. Although the land was slightly smaller, I chose one because I could see the shadow of a tree on the other block of land would give strategic shade over the kitchen of the house of my choice. However, soon after moving in, the other house also sold, and the new neighbour soon removed the tree. Had I made a mistake? I subsequently realised my house was built further towards a side fence, allowing me to extend the house by eight metres. The other house was built in the middle of the property, allowing no room to extend. My property had other advantages too, of which I had no inkling of awareness when I bought it. Was this just good fortune, or was it God subtly guiding my thinking? All I know is that the more I serve God, the more fortunate I become!

At other times, God will allow us to go through very 'deep waters' of potentially disastrous events. But God assures that he is always available to help. He notes, in Isaiah 30:21 (NKJV) **"If you wander from the right path, either to the right or to the left, you will hear a voice behind you** saying, **"You should go this *way*. *Here* is the right *way*."** This 'voice' is usually through the conscience.

Philippians 2:13 (NIV) reminds us," **for it is God who works in you to will and to act in order to fulfill his good purpose".** Who can comprehend the thoughts and persuasions that change our minds? It is humanly impossible to minutely follow God's steps and processes, but certainly, no person will have the excuse to stand before God and plead umbrage.

This, however, is merely the beginning: We have entered through the gates of God's glorious provision, awaiting Jesus to honour his promise to collect us and transfer us bodily into the Kingdom of Gold, or Theology. And so, it is necessary to look beyond the cross of salvation and into the empty tomb and to realise why Christ has risen from the dead and what it means for us.

Green Sanctification (Refining your endeavours)

So far, of the five colours of the Gospel, we have seen God's kingdom, the colour gold; Satan's kingdom, the colour black; the means of escaping Satan's kingdom, the colour red; the amazing beauty of salvation, the colour white; and now, finally, we come to the colour green.

Green is mainly about the conscience and the changing of our mindset to imitate Christ's example. He conscience is an amazing entity being the link between the infinite God and each one of around nine billion people. How it works is described by God to a young man named Cain, in the first book of the Bible, Genesis chapter 4:7. Here, he explained that when you do what is right you will feel elated, but if you do what is wrong, beware! Sin is lining up to devour you, and by ignoring it, it will constantly weigh on your mind and will remove you from God's instruction and encouragement. Actually, we read in 1 Timothy 1:19 that is will actually shipwreck all hope you ever had of finding joy and peace.

Romans 8:16 assures us that God's Spirit joins with our spirit to affirm we are God's children. That assurance registers on or through our conscience, forming a sense of constant joy and expectation.

Paying attention to our conscience is vital for daily tasks. Imagine a huge funnel channelling information into a narrow spout. Anything received – through reading, listening to others, observing God working, preaching, listening to smutty jokes, gossiping, thinking about sexual exploits, or anything else that enters the funnel edge that makes up our existence, trickles down to the spout of our mind, and confuses our conscience. This affects our worldview and thinking processes.

Our spiritual understanding is strangled by condoned and unconfessed sin. Unguarded participation in uncouth situations will also impede wholesome communication with God blocking the sweet, life-giving communication we would otherwise enjoy. The Bible tells me if I regard sin in my heart God will not hear me, and conversely, I will not hear from God. My conscience will weigh heavily on my wellbeing, keeping me in a mental prison.

Our conscience will tell us when we have done wrong in God's view – and even when we have done wrong to others. We just can't quite feel rest assured. Badgering thoughts bombard us. Sometimes thoughts may accuse us even from our earliest memories! In these cases, we must make right with God and make amends with those we have offended, so much as we are able. 1 John 1:9 tells us that if we confess our sin, God is faithful and just to forgive us and cleanse us from every wrong action and thought. PARA.

As weeds to the garden, so is sin to our lives. By ignoring just one sin, we can soon be overwhelmed by a prolificacy of incalculable error. Undoubtedly, thoughts and attitudes are the largest source of error in our lives. No wonder Paul exhorts in 2 Corinthians 10:5, to take every thought captive to the obedience of Christ. It's a big job to stay on top of our thoughts and attitudes, and it's a large part of 'daily bearing your cross'. (Mat 16:24). This means successfully dealing with every incident and thought in our daily lives. It is imperative we keep our conscience clear.

In this lifetime, we are all infected with sin. We will never be without sin, and no-one will ever be acceptable to God in their own right. So, in that case, how can we ever find God's kingdom for our lives? This is by only recognising our complete failure and acknowledging our total dependency on God's grace and seeking God's forgiveness.

Consider for a moment, how film and sound from outer space can arrive at the same time. Sound, which travels at speeds of feet per second, can be wrapped up in light, and travel millions of miles per second through space, at the same speed. Similarly, it is only when we, who at best operate at the speed of sound, are wrapped up 'in Christ' will we ever behold God as friend, and sin will not affect our eternity. A guilty conscience will impede our progress. We must be part of Christ, forgiven, aware of Christ's leading and example, and focused on Christ to be a new creation. Therefore, we do not allow the knowledge of our daily errors to discourage our immediate expectancy of Christ's return.

Eph 2:8-10

God saved you by his grace when you believed. And you can't take credit for this; it is a gift from God.

Salvation is not a reward for the good things we have done, so none of us can boast about it.

For we are God's masterpiece. He has created us anew in Christ Jesus, so we can do the good things he planned for us long ago. NLT

As can be seen from the above scriptures, God has a specific plan for each individual. It is beyond the scope of a natural person to comprehend that plan until they discover the reality of God's presence. It is probably easier to understand through the following picture metaphor:

If we were to build a sailing dinghy, there are necessary factors that must be considered. To begin with, it needs to be constructed from waterproof marine ply as opposed to structural ply. It should be held together with impermeable glue and non-rust screws. It will need a retractable encased daggerboard that extends at least the depth of the vessel, below the vessel. This is imperative for steering and preventing the vessel from sliding sideways in the wind. Cleats screwed either side of the deck will enable the sheets – ropes that hold the foresail in place, making sure the sail is in the best position to use the force of the wind for maximum performance.

There are obviously many, many more factors to consider, but for the purpose of this illustration these will do.

Now, in the NKJV bible 1 Thes. Verse 4, Paul exhorts us to 'know how to possess your own vessel'. The NLT version describes this as 'controlling your own body'. This is referring to having total control over every aspect of our lives – physical, mental and spiritual. So, we are given the task of floating our 'vessel' or existence within the sea of sin and error that currently floods the world system. (By the way, all timber vessels will leak a little water, just as we all will sin in attitude, reaction, demeanour, thought, speech etc. God reminds us to come before him, confess our error, and he promises to forgive us. The more we acknowledge and abide in the reality of his presence, the less we will make mistakes.)

2 Peter chapter 1:3-9 give us specific instruction regarding the building of the vessel of our lives. The quick interpretation of this is to make sure we are living morally, wisely, and being mindful of other people. The metaphorical 'daggerboard' of our lives regards moral excellence to prevent our sliding across or overlooking sin and error.

This leads us directly to the reason God relegated Lucifer to take up residence on the earth, as mentioned above under 'Black – Depravity'. The Bible notes that God wants everyone to be with him in eternity, but he doesn't want programmed servants. He wants those who voluntarily select to be with him. No human can see or perceive God the Father through natural means but has to grow and understand the things of God by faith. Faith is an expectant hope based on a sure outcome. God's word and promises are sure because he cannot lie. The absolute precision of physical laws proves he cannot lie. Physical laws cannot change – If we drop a brick on our foot, it will always hit its target! Even If we jump off a roof, we will never be able to fly. The sun will always rise in the east and set in the west.

The questions above, regarding why Satan, or Lucifer, was banished to earth to God's masterpiece creation is that Satan's depraved nature is ideal for putting mere humans under immense and unrelenting pressure and anguish. But Satan was not given open license to test God's people beyond their ability to resist. The book of Isaiah reveals that God purposely set up the tribulation vehicle in chapter 54 verse 16 but qualifies in verse 17 that the whole reason is to train us for victory and success.

This is verified in the book of Job chapter 1 verses 6-12, where Satan is required to describe his proposed plan to God, who allows or disallows its fulfilment. God transforms Satan's evil planning for his own purposes, which is demonstrated in Daniel 3 verses 12-28. This shows where three of God's people were thrown into an extremely hot fire to destroy them and their godly beliefs. On this occasion, an angel (perhaps Jesus?) visibly appeared to stand alongside them, and they survived without the slightest evidence of Satan's attacks. Similarly, God will stand with us, and between whatever we face. We may be required to endure trying experiences, but we will be delivered from the intended consequence.

Jesus later highlighted the inevitability of this trial process by confirming that all will suffer persecution and problems, Paul also acknowledged its purpose, describing how the experience of pressurised tribulation in one's own earthly life can be useful helping others in similar circumstances.[cxxxviii]

Jesus promised that at the right moment he would return to collect his followers, effectively and bodily removing them from the white and green stages in the kingdom of Depravity and transferring them into the gold-coloured kingdom of Theology which will rule the world.

The conscience is an amazing God Positioning System (GPS). God said that he has written his (moral) laws on every heart. I recall watching a toddler intending to damage a poster. After scattering pamphlets all over the floor, he first held out his hands towards the poster, then looked guiltily around his surrounds to see if anyone was watching, before commencing his plan of action. He obviously knew that what he was planning to do would be wrong. The conscience works from a very young age. It is also the means by which the Holy Spirit checks us against wrong-doing and provides a guide through life. By ignoring their conscience, many have shipwrecked their faith and even their lives.[cxxxix]

It's the conscience that produces feelings of right and wrong, good and bad, fair and unfair.

The Plan

God loves you but…

The above discourse regards our necessary actions and attitudes to please and reach God. This section regards our lives from God's point of view.

God has a definite plan and his intentions and purposes for each one of us is laid out in the Book of Ezekiel, chapter 47. Here life is depicted as a river, flowing in the Spirit of God, verses three to five deal with both physical and spiritual maturity in this river of life. Physically, one normally starts as an infant getting their feet wet in the matters of the world, learning how to master and cope with a variety of situations, learning how to feed and dress themselves, being instructed regarding self-care and relationship to peers.

From there they progress to being knee-deep in the river of life, learning how to successfully manage relationships, learning to negotiate with others. The next stage is being waist deep in the river – adolescence growing in strength and confidence, learning how to succeed and plan, usually with competent instructors. Finally, strong support underfoot is lost, and one must swim with confidence, experiential know-how, and advice in the river of the Spirit of life.

Spiritually, one goes through exactly the same stages of learning the basic tenets of Christianity, experiencing the comfort of fellowship with other Christians, learning to relate to God and his people, before finally launching into the reality of God's presence, where the Holy Spirit gives the bulk of instruction.[cxl]

Verses eight to ten of Ezekiel chapter 47 address the effectiveness of one's survival in the waters of life. By holding a firm position in the centre of God's plan for one's physical and spiritual life, their ability to attract others, as well as bring fresh thinking and influence into stagnant, and murky situations will succeed abundantly. They will inspire others to be more active in life's successes.

Verse eleven shows that those who resist God's intentions, always seeking the boundaries of how far out they can legitimately live, will remain unchanged, merely eddying in the mundaneness of life, bumping from one problem to the next along the rocks of adversity. But success in the river of life, says verse twelve, will result in affecting unimaginable lifelong wealth.

We are reminded in 1 Corinthians 2:9 that what God has planned for us – physically and spiritually, has never entered the human mind or comprehension! We have no idea what God will allow into our lives apart from our own expectations. Very often, amazing changes of circumstances may be experienced with God's direct intervention injected into our lives: depending on His purposes – such as with the Apostle Paul's wake-up call, mentioned in Part 1, 'A Change of Track.'

Part A – Adam to the Day of the Lord

Another vital clue in God's overall plan is revealed in Revelation 13:8 which speaks of 'the Lamb (Christ) slain from the foundation of the earth.' NKJV. God pre-planned that Jesus should die on behalf of mankind! The NLT version describes this passage as, 'the Book of Life before the world was made – the Book that belongs to the Lamb who was slaughtered.'

Either way, the implication advances the idea that everything was planned before the world was made. Christ was destined to die before anything else even existed. It also implies that the name of every person who ever lived or still lives was written in the Book of Life! God planned from eternity past, that everyone in all creation should be redeemed![cxli] However, both interpreted versions reveal that anyone whose name does not appear in that book will go into an eternity of suffering along with the rest of Satan's depraved world.

There appears to be no scripture instructing me to 'get your name written into the book.' So, obviously, our names pre-exist in the book; we need to ensure they are not removed! Both NKJV and NLT record that God would blot out or erase the name from under heaven of all those who spurn his provision for salvation.[cxlii] Revelation 3:5 shows that all who are victorious in salvation and overcome through the challenges of life will not have their names removed. But those who disregard God's provision and ignore his standards will join the finalisation of the kingdom of Depravity.

"Life is not meant to be easy, my child; but take courage; it can be delightful."[xliii]

Malevolence is an integral part of life: everyone has good times and challenging times. Some challenges result from our own foolish behaviours and some are God-ordered to open our eyes to our faults and errors, and also to open our eyes to possibilities. The only way to have constant and continuous joy is to remain in close fellowship with Jesus Christ; even then, there will be challenging moments! Our eventual outcome will always rest on personal choices. Tribulation is reminiscent of being an object floating on the sea of life. Huge, crashing waves have the potential to drive us deep beyond the surface of comfort, but depending on how soon after we seek God will determine how quickly we return to the surface again. Unfortunately, if we continue to turn away from God, we will never re-surface!

Part B In training – Regardless, you are going to hurt.

Scripture remains unclear as to why God has specifically decided to train us through tribulation. Although, we can logically work out that strength of character and resolve, are defined under pressure. Determination and loyalty are also tested in this manner; an easy life will not develop resolve. However, attentiveness often shortens these times of tribulation because once the lesson is learned we, hopefully, move beyond the specific problem, and God re-arranges our situation. If we have learned the lesson, it is pointless to continue. Although the lesson is reinforced when similar situations recur from time to time.

I have noticed that by trying to avoid dealing with a difficult situation usually causes the ethereal structure of the issue to follow you where-ever you go. Even to another country!

This is what the Lord says – your Redeemer, the
Holy One of Israel:
I am the Lord your God,
who teaches you what is good for you
and leads you along the paths you should follow.[cxliv]

So it basically begs the question: How quickly do we learn?

Verse 20 of Romans chapter one informs us that the invisible attributes of God's power and divine nature can be clearly seen by the natural things around us. For example, we eat food to sustain our lives, but Jesus told us we do not survive exclusively by eating food but by God's word, which sustains all people, both good and bad. Obviously, he was not talking of our natural lives, but of our eternal lives. Proverbs chapter seventeen reminds us that God tests our hearts – not that He wants to evaluate us. He already knows all about us. No, He wants us to have an honest evaluation of ourselves! In the garden of Eden God asked, 'Adam where are you?' He knew where Adam was, but He wanted Adam to know and question his own situation. Perhaps, we can better understand these spiritual principles by observing our natural teaching methods:

For infants we give them small challenges and encouragement to develop their skills of crawling, walking, running, jumping, kicking, throwing and catching.[cxlv] As they grow, we may set up obstacle courses to develop climbing and outdoor skills. We encourage them and teach them to reason and calculate. We give them "mine/not mine" games to develop honesty. We challenge them to reach beyond what they currently master. As their brains develop, we give them scenarios to exercise their reasoning and endurance skills, as well as constantly training their awareness of morals. In time they eventually decide they are autonomous, needing less and less parental guidance and we trust that they will behave responsibly, seeking their own way through life.

In exactly the same way, as new-born Christians, Peter instructs us to strongly desire the Milk of the Word,[cxlvi] and to the book of Hebrews recipients Paul advises progression to maturity, after learning the basics of turning away from destroying practices and habits, learning to have faith and trust in God, knowing about the various baptisms, having authority over things in which we are concerned, being raised from death, the penalty of ignoring God, and pressing on until God changes the situations in our lives.[cxlvii]

God planned our training and acknowledged that this duration on earth was going to be full of tribulation and hard times. Jesus didn't infer that tribulation *might* occur but rather spoke about *when* tribulation or persecution occurs. During the last three years of his earthly sojourn, much of his speaking was about tribulation – especially that directed towards his own followers! In fact, Jesus openly told his disciples that they will definitely have tribulation in this world, but to "cheer up because he has overcome the world". It's part of our training. It gives us a choice to either turn to God or away from God. Either we turn to God and work out how to climb out of our suffocating hole or turn our backs on God and never find lasting peace and relief.

Paul acknowledges the truth of universal suffering when, after being stoned to death for his witness, but miraculously recovering, exhorts the disciples, saying that 'we must (go) through many tribulations (to) enter the Kingdom of God.'(NKJV)[cxlviii] Paul also reveals the purpose of tribulation, saying '**Problems and trials help us develop endurance, strength of character, and a positive and confident hope of salvation.**'[cxlix]

James outrightly writes,

'Consider troubles an opportunity for great joy so that your faith can be tested, and your endurance can grow, until you are perfect and complete, in need of

nothing. **(NLT) If you are perplexed, ask God to help
you and he will without rebuke.**^{xl}

God assures us of his purpose and intention of allowing hard times
in our lives. He states,

**'I create the blacksmith
who fires up his forge
and makes weapons designed to kill.
I also create the destroyer –
But no weapon that can hurt you has ever been forged.
Any accuser who takes you to court will be
dismissed as a liar.
This is what God's servants can expect.
I'll see to it that everything works out for the best.**^{xli}

Here God reveals he has knowingly allowed trouble and challenging
circumstances to expressly put each of us under pressure. But He qualifies
his reasoning to show, regardless of the situation, his intention is to train
us to overcome. Experience tells us such ordeals can often be brutal,
making it imperative to fix our mind on God and wait with child-like
expectancy, anticipating that God will respond on our behalf. God loves
to help and direct.

Extreme times are not only reserved for personal challenges. Nations
also go through a training program. Isaiah speaks about desolation,
destruction, famine, and war sent against the nation of Israel. And in
another chapter God bemoans their destruction, by saying,

**'Oh, that you had listened to my commands! Then
you would have had peace flowing like a gentle**

**river, and righteousness rolling over you like waves
in the sea. There would have been no need for your
destruction.**[xlii]

Similar descriptions of malevolent agents are sounded in Revelation chapter 6:2-8, which makes us realise these forces were originally released with the advent of original sin. They were first mentioned in Genesis chapter four verse eight, when Cain, the first child born, murdered his brother. Many places of the Old Testament, as well as recorded secular history, depict these terrifying forces at work around the world, all the time! And the amazing truth is that they were acknowledged from the Throne of God! They serve a purpose.

We therefore conclude that life has been set up for us to grope our way to finding God's pre-arranged plan for each of our lives. He declares he will never leave us, but is freely available, ready to advise, assist, correct and encourage. Whatever is required to build us into qualified victors. Wrong choices merely mean we have a deeper hole out of which to climb. God will never abandon us, whatever we choose – right or wrong! We must however, never, ever give up looking to and expecting God to help in our daily challenges.

Part C – The Final Touch, or the second centimetre of our tape measure

Scripture reveals little about life on Earth after Jesus returns, but there is enough to draw a hazy picture. To begin with, Nebuchadnezzar's prophetic dream depicted earth's historic dominant rulers from Israel's perspective. Visualised as a statue, it descended in quality, from Babylon as the head of gold, followed by Medes and Persians, Greeks, Romans, and finishing at the feet with a strong/weak conglomeration of European/

Middle Eastern countries with faulty perceptions,[cliii] depicted as a mixture of iron and clay. The final mixture of world rulers is pure clay.

From the depiction in the book of Daniel chapter two, through God's eyes we can observe the gradual inevitable collapse of moral values. Oh, there's nothing new about any of it. Immorality has always impacted human existence, but the scope of and indifference to moral pollution by current world leaders and society has never been so prevalent as today. Surely God views the quality of our current general worldview as clay, with occasional pockets of iron: sexual perversion is barely challenged today – rather, in many circles, it's even preferred!

God told Abraham that he was to wait out four generations until the distasteful practises of the nations in Canaan matured, before Abraham could possess the land.[cliv] Leviticus 18 states that the total destruction of these people sprang from their perverse practices. Seemingly, we have apparently reached a similar abhorrent stage in about one generation!

Christ's return, portrayed as transcendent, unyielding, and without human input (a stone cut without hands) will completely remove all trace of the former juggernauts of world history, and will have a growing universal influence.

At the time of Christ's return nuclear weapons will apparently be employed. This is because seven months will be required to bury the dead; any bones discovered thereafter will not be touched but visibly marked for special teams to handle. There is also indication that the elements of the sky will be burned away, but whether or not this is caused transcendently or by nuclear means is not stipulated - only that it will happen![clv]

The earth will be impacted by incredible changes. There will be no sea, sun or moon,[clvi] and there will be direct communication with Heaven. We are given an example of such an occurrence when Jacob dreamed of angels ascending and descending on a stairway to Heaven, and correspondingly, we can expect similar direct communication with God in Heaven, probably on a daily or instant occurrence. The glory of God will produce earth's light and will suffice every nation. Entry into God's city will be restricted only to those whose names are written in the Book of Life. Those who steadfastly ignore their God-created conscience and morals, can never enter.

In three places the Bible mentions 'outer darkness'. Apparently, this differs from the 'Lake of Fire' reserved for Satan and his angels as well as those that reject God's incredible offer of salvation. Now, 'outer darkness', listed in most Bible translations and simply called 'darkness' in the NIV, could possibly refer to the antithesis of geographical Jerusalem. This would be away from the glory of the Celestial City of Jerusalem – the opposite side of the world.

The accuracy of the following statement is difficult to imagine. Matthew 25:14-30 seems to imply the fate of those Christians who chose not to apply themselves to their utmost in serving God. The lazy servant was sent to 'outer darkness'. Perhaps this means to serve God amongst people full of unhappiness and deep regret on the far side of the world.

Time will change as well, returning to something similar to the portrayal of longevity before the flood. Most of the characters listed in the book of Genesis lived around nine hundred years and we are informed that men will live as long as trees, and to die at a mere one-hundred years would mean they had been cursed. This suggests there will only be one generation during the Millenium – which is the one-thousand-year reign of Christ when he returns.[clvii]

Verses 20-22 of Isaiah 65 seem to suggest the business model and the need for employment will cease, but everyone will manage their own lives and be self-contained. All aggression and hurt will cease – even possible harm, such as snake bite or dangerous animals will no longer occur. Children will at last be completely safe.

Summary

Biblical prophecy will be finally and completely fulfilled: Jesus is returning soon to earth to collect his faithful and expectant followers, and end Christianity.

But will you be ready?

Bibliography and Endnotes

i   https://www.brainyquote.com/authors/herbert-a-simon-quotes

ii   Bosworth FF – Christ the Healer

iii   Wilde Robert History Expert M.A., Medieval Studies, Sheffield University, B.A., Medieval Studies, Sheffield University, Robert Wilde is a historian who writes about European history. He is the author of the History in an Afternoon textbook series. Updated on May 05, 2019

iv   Pro 14:21

v   Sinek Simon on Millennials in the Workplace – YouTube

vi   Tristate Livestock News: Food control: Dutch farming on the verge of a disaster as government pushes to close 3,000 farms

vii Remsburg Geoff. https://finance.yahoo.com/news/government-control-over-money-233253599.html

viii Harari Yuval Noah. YouTube 'AI and the Future of Humanity'-Yuval Noah Harari at the Frontiers Forum April , 29, 2023, in Montreux, Switzerland

ix   2 Tim 1:9 (NLT)

x   Mat 24:22

xi   Joh 14:3

xii Pro 29:18 NLT

xiii Wikipedia: s.v. 'Tower of Babel' 01:47, 21 November 2023 HeyElliott talk contribs

xiv Gen. 12:2–3. NLT

xv God never leaves himself without a witness, and the following sites contain interesting information on the subject. Gerald Flurry, Philadelphia Trumpet – https://www.thetrumpet.com/18698-sodom-and-gomorrah- proved
Ross Patterson, 'Sodom & Gomorrah – True Location Found,' YouTube video, https://www.youtube.com/watch?v=KBCs4wexgRk.

xvi   Isa 42:8

xvii   Heb 11:19

xviii   Numbers 1:46

xix   Rom. 3:20, Gal. 3:24.

xx   Prov. 19:16.

xxi   Dennis Prager, 'Do Not Misuse God's Name,' https://www.prageru.com/video/do-not-misuse-gods-name/ (transcript available).

xxii   Exo 20:1–17 (PARA).

xxiii   Mat 6:14,15

xxiv   Lev. 10:1–3 (PARA).

xxv   Prov. 3:3 (PARA).

xxvi   Matt. 22:37–40.

xxvii   C. S. Lewis, *Mere Christianity*. Used with permission.

xxviii   Exo. 34:6,7 para

xxix   Exo 12:31-36

xxx   1 Kin 18:21 NLT

xxxi   Exo 32:8

xxxii   Exo 19:16-19

xxxiii   Amos 8:11.

xxxiv   Wikipedia: s.v. 'Pharisees & Sadducees | Definition, Beliefs & Differences'

xxxv   Deu 4:26-28show page numbers

xxxvi   read Amos chapter 4 and Zec 11 in the Message Bible

xxxvii   Zec 11:6, 9-12

xxxviii   Mat 23:38

xxxix   Exo 39:7

xl   Exo 29:33 Lev 21:10

xli   Mat 27:51 Mark 15:38

xlii   Luk 22:20, Joh 19:30

xliii   Rom 11:8

xliv   Matthew 16:24 NLT

xlv   John 16:33 NLT

xlvi   1 Cor. 9: 9–10 NLT.

xlvii   Col. 2:23 NLT.

xlviii   2 Cor 3:7-8

xlix   Mat 24:9-14

l   Luk 21:24

li   R. C. Sproul, "Caring for Widows," Ligonier, January 25, 2017, www.ligonier.org/learn/articles/caring-widows.

lii   Exod. 22:22–23.

liii   Rom. 14:7.

liv   Deut. 28:13.

lv   2 Peter 1:4.

lvi   Christian History Institute, "Pliny's Letter to Trajan," study module 102, https://christianhistoryinstitute.org/study/module/pliny.

lvii   Paul Keresztes, 'Marcus Aurelius a Persecutor?' *Harvard Theological Review* 61, no. 3 (July 1968): 321–341.

lviii   Diocletian is probably the most persecuting of all the Roman emperors, but Galerius, though an antagonist to Christianity, ended the Diocletianic Persecution by issuing an "edict of tolerance." Wikipedia sv 'Diocletian Persecution' https://en.wikipedia.org/w/index.php?title=Diocletianic_Persecution&oldid=1158999753

lix   Shushma Malik and Caillan Davenport, 'Mythbusting Ancient Rome – Throwing Christians to the Lions,' The University of Queensland School of Historical and Philosophical Inquiry (November 22, 2016), https://hpi.uq.edu.au/article/2016/11/mythbusting-ancient-rome-%E2%80%93-throwing-christians-lions.

lx   Wikipedia, s.v. 'Pope,' last modified August 11, 2022, 10:20, https://en.wikipedia.org/wiki/Pope#Title_and_etymology.

lxi   Smith, Gary, 'The History of the Catholic Church in Latin America and Liberation Theology', Yale New Haven Teachers institute, 1982 Volume V > Unit 7 (82.05.07)

lxii   Brittanica, 'Western Schism', Last Updated: Jan 11, 2024

lxiii   Wikipedia, s.v 'Pope Urban II' 00:22, 14 June 2023 GreenC bot talk contribs

lxiv   2 Cor. 5:8.

lxv   https://www.britannica.com/topic/Spanish-Inquisition

lxvi   Wikipedia, s.v. 'Christianity in the Middle Ages' 07:30, 10 May 2023 Iskandar323

lxvii   https://www.history.com/topics/renaissance/renaissance. History.com Editors. April 20, 2023

lxviii   https://www.history.com/topics/religion/reformation. History.com Editors April 11,2019

lxix   https://www.bl.uk/shakespeare/articles/key-features-of-renaissance-culture

lxx   Phillips, Charles. https://www.scotland.org.uk/history/killing-time; "Massacre at Béziers". *Encyclopedia Britannica*, 14 Jul. 2022; wiki s.v. Massacre of Verden 17:11, 21 April 2023 2a02:aa1:1023:ad70:10ff:60d:fca2:652f

lxxi   Wikipedia: s.v. 'History of Protestantism' 13:37, 20 December 2023 Ebbedlila talk contribs

lxxii   Britannica, The Editors of Encyclopaedia. "John Wesley". Encyclopedia Britannica, 22 Dec. 2023, https://www.britannica.com/biography/John-Wesley. Accessed 31 January 2024.

lxxiii Missouri State500 Years of Reformations — and Their Books **The Baptist Tradition**

lxxiv 1 Cor. 4:6

lxxv http://hobart.k12.in.us/ksms/worldreligions/Christian/denominations

lxxvi https://logosseminaryguide.com/alphabetical-list-of-denominations/

lxxvii 1 Cor. 12:4.

lxxviii Much of the above is based on my own observations over nearly 70 years.

lxxix ttps://www.theguardian.com/world/from-the-archive-blog/2020/oct/07/birth-of-belgium-october-1830-

lxxx Wikipedia, s.v. 'British Empire' 10:55, 25 June 2023 Juan Miguel U. Palero

lxxxi https://courses.lumenlearning.com/atd-herkimer-westerncivilization/chapter/the-development-of-papal-supremacy/

lxxxii This saying has also been attributed to the Greek philosopher Aristotle.

lxxxiii Eliza Rosenberg, "Faith Divided," Christian History Institute, https://christianhistoryinstitute.org/magazine/article/faith-divided.

lxxxiv Jonathan Riley-Smith, *The First Crusade and the Idea of Crusading* (Philadelphia: University of Pennsylvania Press, 1986).

lxxxv Paul Johnson, *A History of Christianity* (New York: Atheneum, 1977), 490.

lxxxvi C. S. Lewis, *The Problem of Pain*, chapter 6 (used by permission).

lxxxvii Most of this information was gleaned from various Wikipedia sites regarding American settlements.

lxxxviii https://en.wikipedia.org/w/index.php?title=Spanish_colonization_of_the_Americas&oldid=1160018140

lxxxix https://study.com/learn/lesson/puritans-america-beliefs-history-leaders.html

xc https://en.wikipedia.org/w/index.php?title=Women_of_Colonial_Virginia&oldid=1154018747
https://en.wikipedia.org/w/index.php?title=History_of_women_in_the_United_States&oldid=1160368146

xci https://en.wikipedia.org/w/index.php?title=Dutch_colonization_of_the_Americas&oldid=1152031045

xcii https://study.com/learn/lesson/puritans-america-beliefs-history-leaders.html (why did the puritans leave England)

xciii https://journals.sagepub.com/doi/pdf/10.1177/2396939319880074

xciv Jer 31:33

xcv https://www.nps.gov/wamo/index.htm

xcvi https://mariomurillo.org/2022/11/12/christianity-will-survive-without-america-but-america-will-not-survive-without-christianity/

xcvii Luke 21:28. PARA

xcviii Mark 4:29 NLT.

xcix   Joh 14:1-3

c   https://www.thegospelcoalition.org/themelios/review/mission-in-the-old-testament-israel-as-a-light-to-the-nations/

ci   Isa 66:19

cii   Rom 11:1 NKJV

ciii   Rom 11:25,26 NLT

civ   Mat 23:38,39 NLT

cv   Rev 7 and Rev 14 probably refer to the Jewish evangelists

cvi   2 Pet 3:12 NLT

cvii   2Thes 2:11

cviii   1 Joh 2:18-22, 1 Joh 4:3, 2 The 2:3

cix   Jer 30:7

Part 2

cx   Dan 11:41

cxi   Ecc 3:11

cxii   Jam 1:14,15 Phi 4:8

cxiii   Joh 14:6

cxiv   Exo 34:6,7 NLT

cxv   Dennis Prager, 'Do Not Misuse God's Name,' https://www.prageru.com/video/do-not-misuse-gods-name/ (transcript available).

cxvi   Exo 20:1–17. PARA for simpler understanding

cxvii   Mat 5:45 NIV

cxviii   Isa 60:17 NLT

cxix   Rom 3:23 NLT

cxx   1 Cor 2:9 PARA

cxxi   Ecc 3:11

cxxii   Joh 3:5 NLT

cxxiii   2 Pet 1:3-9

cxxiv   https://www.barna.com/research/most-american-christians-do-not-believe-that-satan-or-the-holy-spirit-exist/

cxxv   Hinkley – Gordon B Hinckley - www.goodreads.com/quotes/114894

cxxvi   Rom 7:18-20

cxxvii   Prager, Dennis, 'Happiness is a serious problem', p19, HarperCollins Publishers 1998

cxxviii   Joh 14:6

cxxix   Joh 3:16, Isa 53:6b

cxxx   1Cor 15: 21-23, 45-49

cxxxi   Heb 2:17

cxxxii   Col 2:14

cxxxiii   2Pet 1:4

cxxxiv   Col 1:13

cxxxv   Rom 10:9

cxxxvi   Gal 3:27

cxxxvii   2Cor 5:17 PARA

cxxxviii   2 cor 1:3-5

cxxxix   1 Tim 1:19,20

cxl   1 Cor 2:13

cxli   2 Pet 3:9

cxlii   Deu 29:20

cxliii   Shaw, George Bernard – featured in: George Bernard Shaw Quotes

cxliv   Isa 48:17 NLT

cxlv   https://www.napacentre.com.au/obstacle-course-ideas/

cxlvi   1Pet 2:2

cxlvii   Heb 6:1-3

cxlviii   Acts 14:22 NKJV

cxlix   Rom 5:3-5 NLT

cl   Jam 1:2-5 PARA

cli   Isa 54:16,17 MSG

clii   Isa 48:18,19 NLT

cliii   Dan 1:31-33

cliv   Gen 15:16

clv   Eze 39:9-15

clvi   Isa 60:19,20

clvii   Isa 65:20-25

www.ingramcontent.com/pod-product-compliance
Lightning Source LLC
Chambersburg PA
CBHW030316130626
46549CB00002B/877

9 781966 652182